WOODCOCK
FIELDCRAFT AND QUARRY

WOODCOCK
FIELDCRAFT AND QUARRY

PROFESSOR COLIN TROTMAN

Quiller

Copyright © 2010 Colin Trotman

First published in the UK in 2010
by Quiller, an imprint of Quiller Publishing Ltd

British Library Cataloguing-in-Publication Data
A catalogue record for this book
is available from the British Library

ISBN 978 1 84689 052 9

The right of Colin Trotman to be identified as the author of this work has been asserted in accordance with the Copyright, Design and Patent Act 1988.

The information in this book is true and complete to the best of our knowledge. All recommendations are made without any guarantee on the part of the Publisher, who also disclaims any liability incurred in connection with the use of this data or specific details.

All rights reserved. No part of this book may be reproduced or transmitted in any form or by any means, electronic or mechanical including photocopying, recording or by any information storage and retrieval system, without permission from the Publisher in writing.

Photographs by the author, except where stated: all photographs copyright of the photographer.

Book and jacket design by Sharyn Troughton

Printed in China

Quiller
An imprint of Quiller Publishing Ltd
Wykey House, Wykey, Shrewsbury, SY4 1JA
Tel: 01939 261616 Fax: 01939 261606
E-mail: info@quillerbooks.com
Website: www.countrybooksdirect.com

Contents

	Dedication	6
	Acknowledgements	7
	Introduction	9
CHAPTER 1	Woodcock Today	15
CHAPTER 2	Natural History	20
CHAPTER 3	Migration	46
CHAPTER 4	Fieldcraft and Woodcock Shooting	74
CHAPTER 5	Tools for the job	89
CHAPTER 6	From the Field to the Table	125
CHAPTER 7	Future Woodcock	139
	Conclusion	167
	Bibliography	171
	Index	174

Dedication

To my wife Sian for allowing me more space and time to indulge my love of woodcock and woodcock hunting than one man probably deserves. To Jacob, Caitlin and Hannah for reminding me, through their eyes, how wonderful and rewarding nature and the countryside are, how precious they are and how we must protect our heritage.

Acknowledgements

I have received great support from many people at the different stages of writing this book. Above all else, that of my wife Sian for her unstinting faith in me, her advice, support and encouragement. A calming and wise influence in a sometimes stormy sea!

My thanks to my good friends Brian Evans, Dr Jean Paul Boidot, Dr Mike Swan and Dr Yves Ferrand for willingly sharing with me their knowledge and passion for woodcock. I am grateful to Ray Lockyer, Paul Leyshon, Dr Jean Paul Boidot, Tony Kieran, Tom Mptelas and Simon Rees for supplying some of the photographs so important for this book. I am grateful also to Andrew Hoodless, Roy Dennis, Felipe Diaz and Mark Hinge for allowing me to use their materials here. Also, my thanks to Alma Frazer and Andrew Thorpe of the North Sea Bird Club for sharing their records with me.

My thanks especially to former editor of *Shooting Times*, Robert Gray, for encouraging and publishing my early attempts and to current Editor Camilla Clark and Deputy Editor Alastair Balmain for agreeing that I could reproduce some of the material from my articles for *Shooting Times* in this book. Also thanks to my good friend, the chef Mark Hinge, for permission to reproduce some of his recipes, in Chapter 6, which were originally published within the pages of *Shooting Times*.

Particular thanks to Ray Devine, Des Crofton and Barry Sullivan of the National Association of Regional Game Councils of Ireland (NARGC) for assisting me so willingly and for agreeing that I could reproduce the NARGC data on woodcock shot in Ireland. From elsewhere in Ireland I have been privileged to receive the long-term support of woodcock 'aficionados' Darrin Gardiner, John Bourke and Dave Egan. From Wales, I must acknowledge the willingness of Michael Williams of the Camddwr Shooting Society and Roger Evans from Narberth to help and give advice whenever asked to do so. I was greatly encouraged by my fellow officers of the Welsh Woodcock Club, Lyn

Murley, Simon Rees, Mike Thomas Palmer, Peter Jones, Eifion Williams and Oliver West.

Two people above all others share my passion and concern for woodcock, namely, Michael MacKenzie from the Eilean Iarmain shoot on the Isle of Skye and Mike Appleby from the Honeycombe Shoot in Dorset. It is fitting that they are both Head Keepers who truly appreciate this sporting bird and reflect this in their practice. Many thanks.

My appreciation to that great organiser of a rough shooting day, Eifion Williams, for many superb days in the field hunting woodcock. A truly superb woodcock shot and great sportsman. To Gwynlais Williams and Colin Jones who make up the other members of 'the team of three' mentioned in these pages: thank you for your company.

Thanks also to Liz Whitwell for her unending advice and support on all matters of an IT nature.

Finally, I must acknowledge my late father Cecil Trotman who not only encouraged wholeheartedly and with much visible pride and pleasure all that I did in the shooting and fishing world through my boyhood, teenage years and into adulthood, but also implanted in my psyche for ever, the value of all living things and our responsibility not to squander their lives. Thanks Dad.

Colin Trotman

Introduction

The woodcock *(Scolopax rusticola)* is much revered and held in high esteem across the nations of Europe. It appears in poetry and literature from the early middle ages onwards. Richard J. Ussher [1903: 247] draws our attention to the fact that the native Celtic people have a long-standing awareness of and relationship to the woodcock. He cites Gerald Cambrensis – known also as Gerald the Welshman, a great scholar and lawmaker of his day – who appears to have been a keen observer of woodcock also. Eight hundred years ago, in the twelfth century, he noted on his Christian pilgrimage to spread the Gospel throughout Ireland that there were 'immense flights of snipes...both the larger species of the woods and the smaller of the marches'. He clearly meant the woodcock and the common snipe. For, the woodcock is enshrined in the Celts' native Gaelic tongues; Cymraeg (Welsh) and Breton; it is known as *cyffylog* in Cymraeg/Welsh, *crebhar* in Irish Gaelic, *coileach coille* in Scots Gaelic, *kefeleg* in Breton and as *bécasse* in French. The tribes of both Cymru and Breton had similar names for the woodcock, both derived from the word *ceffyl*, which means horse. The association being that the noise a woodcock makes when flushed, that 'prrr' or 'brrr' noise of threshing wings, is similar to, and can be heard in, the 'snorting' noise a horse frequently makes.

I have a lifetime's fascination with woodcock! At the start of my hunting apprenticeship, before teenage years even, I spent innumerable hours watching for the full moon in late October as this signalled the start of the annual woodcock migration to the British Isles. As a result, I became fascinated by the extraordinary migration routes that these wonderful birds undertake. There is still so much I wish to learn about the woodcock, a sporting bird 'par excellence', the rough shooter's delight. It has been a fascinating exercise and very much a labour of love. There are many, many fantastic sportsmen out there who care dearly for woodcock and their sport with woodcock. They are also a knowledgeable group; many have a lifetime's experience of woodcock, much of which was crafted in the presence of a previous generation of rough shooters.

Much of the documented and published evidence, the perceived wisdom, the gathered knowledge of woodcock has been gleaned from the big shoots owned by the landed gentry mainly in Ireland and England. In fact, the Game Conservancy Trust in England (now renamed the Game and Wildlife Conservation Trust) still estimates migrant woodcock numbers/migrant population trends by using bag records from some of the big organised shoots. This is clearly problematical for a number of reasons. First, big pheasant shoots and woodcock do not mix well. Second, on some of these estates woodcock are passing through as infrequent visitors on their way elsewhere. Now, if anyone seriously wants to know about trends in woodcock numbers, habits and habitats they would be better placed talking to the rough shooters of the Celtic fringes of Wales, Ireland and Scotland. For it is only in these regions that sufficient numbers arrive to allow sportsmen to dedicate their time exclusively to woodcock. The knowledge and bag records of this particular group of sportsmen have been, at best, under-utilised and at worst completely ignored. In my part of the world, for many of us, come mid- to late November, woodcock are the main game. Sportsmen in Ireland, as in Wales and Scotland, know and cherish their woodcock. I have never fully accepted the old adage on woodcock: 'Here today gone tomorrow'! In my experience, once they are on their actual wintering grounds they rarely wander far unless driven to do so by extremes of cold weather patterns. Even then, these are usually just relatively short hops to more favourable, less frost- or ice-ridden levels or regions. In the period late December 2008 running two weeks into January 2009 we had almost four weeks of iron-hard frosts and some significant falls of snow. By the end of the first week, woodcock had shifted to more hospitable areas. By the end of the third week of severe cold weather, they were at sea level and condition-wise were beginning to lose weight. Outside such weather-induced shifts, the old adage merely refers to woodcock in transit. That is, those that rest in particular areas and then proceed to their annual long-stay wintering grounds.

The high point of my shooting season is always the arrival of the woodcock. It has been this way for a very long time and, in fact, from the days of my boyhood forty years and more away. I was brought up in a very keen rough shooting family who depended upon rabbits for their main sport but willingly included any incidentals such as pigeon or duck in their gamebag. In those days, in the early 1960s, pheasants in the rough shooter's bag were as rare as hen's teeth! However, the arrival of woodcock on the October full moon changed all of this. One uncle was a woodcock obsessive. No other person I knew was as excited as he in relation to the October full moon; his only interest in the moon was woodcock-driven, as the moon at that time of the year was his signal that the woodcock would soon arrive. He and I spent much time moon-gazing over many Octobers, impatiently wishing it to turn to full.

Our sporting days were always mixed-bag affairs, but the woodcock held pride of place. Like the sea trout, woodcock favour the oft lovely and isolated landscapes of the western fringes of the British Isles. Whilst, in those days, we usually found ourselves in a 'game-species' barren part of the country, in South Wales, this sport was enhanced significantly with the arrival of the woodcock. In reality, this was the only so-called game bird available to us. Widely dispersed and not simply faithful to the coverts of the big shooting estates, our woodcock were to be found in the small, rough and neglected landscape where more affluent shooters did not bother to go. Our sport was therefore 'rough' indeed, but free and conducted in some of the most stunning scenery imaginable. It was frequently the case that, near mountain streams, where we shot woodcock in the winter, sea trout could be seen spawning in the late autumn. Like sea trout, woodcock, we learned, were often found in the same place, season after season – in the same lie for sea trout and under the same bush for woodcock.

Through sheer necessity, my knowledge of woodcock was honed by first-hand experience of hunting them as an apprentice to my uncles. This involved doing all of the donkey work but learning the craft at the same time. My love of woodcock and my lifelong interest in all aspects of their existence grew out of this. This all-absorbing interest in them has, in fact, been enhanced, and has reached new heights, through the advances of information communication technology. The computer and especially the internet have opened up, literally, a whole world of woodcock. I quickly discovered that 'out there', as it were, there were other woodcock obsessives who shared my hunger for more knowledge of woodcock; for more facts about their lifestyle and needs and – perhaps more importantly – that other people across the world shared my love of woodcock hunting. It is the case that, for people like me, one *hunts* and not simply *shoots* woodcock. In the early years of this new millennium it is very much the case that woodcock remain one of the few truly wild species that we can still hunt. Untouched by the hand of man, the European woodcock *(Scolopax rusticola)* is born in the wilds of north-west Russia or Finland or Sweden and migrates through sheer genetic compulsion to the semi-wild areas of north-west Europe. To the Celtic fringes of Cornwall, Wales, Scotland and Ireland they come year after year and, in my estimation, in increasing numbers. I say this not only from the perspective of a lifelong woodcock shooter, having shot woodcock in England, Wales, Scotland, Ireland and France, but also as someone who has kept a record of every day spent in the field after woodcock. My records clearly show an upward trend in woodcock numbers visiting my part of the British Isles. In addition to this, in 2000 I set up a network of correspondents across the UK, Ireland and Europe to share information and to (generally, but not scientifically), assess trends in woodcock numbers. This I did as a part of my monthly article, The Woodcock Broadcast, for *Shooting Times*.

During the decade prior to writing this, there is a clearly discernible increase in migratory woodcock numbers in the UK and Ireland. There is, I believe, an optimum number of woodcock per acre. Good and precise records of a particular area over a ten-year period will, quite remarkably, reveal a consistency in the numbers of woodcock flushed for particular periods of the season for specific months of the season. In this manner, differing shooting areas become 'twenty woodcock' places or 'thirty woodcock' places or, in the best of examples, 'fifty woodcock' places. Within limits, these are the kind of numbers you would expect to flush when the birds are settled on their wintering grounds.

I am fortunate that I have enough woodcock shooting available to me to only shoot my woodcock places once a month at most, but usually only twice per season. With these relatively long periods of little disturbance, woodcock numbers build to reach an optimum. I firmly believe that woodcock are fully exploiting the availability of good roosting and feeding areas these days, as this optimum number has increased not only since the days of my boyhood but significantly over the last fifteen years. My shooting diaries are more than a record of numbers shot. Far more important for me is the number of woodcock *flushed*. For example, referring back to my earlier claim of remarkable consistency in relation to woodcock numbers, it is a fact that, for the ten-year period 1998–2008, my records show that on average, through my rough shooting activities, I would flush somewhere close to 500 woodcock for the period October 20th–January 31st. In the season 2007–2008 I flushed nearer 1,000 woodcock for exactly the same effort as previous years in terms of hunting days.

I have to admit that, unless I am fully engaged in work-related issues – itself a hard thing to achieve for someone who prefers comfortable shirts and wellingtons as a dress sense statement – or family issues, or fly fishing, then I am thinking woodcock. Whilst driving in the British Isles and north-west France especially, I am constantly spying out 'good' woodcock ground. In the winter months in between my shooting and writing on woodcock I am out most evenings at dusk counting flighting woodcock. To add to my already 'woodcock focused' lifestyle, in 2005 I set up the Welsh Woodcock Club/Clwb Cyffylog Cymru to protect both our sport with woodcock and the woodcock themselves. Be in no doubt that, while many leading authorities on woodcock agree that numbers are stable and even on the increase; while people like myself are prepared to claim that woodcock are, in fact, the sporting quarry success story of our time, there are those who are eager to curtail and even end our hunting of them. The opportunity to focus exclusively on woodcock is very much the privileged position of rough shooters and some commercial interests on the western edges of Britain and Ireland. We are thus a minority group who will be 'picked-off' unless we get our act together and unite in our concern for hunting woodcock and woodcock conservation.

This is, therefore, not just a book on shooting or hunting woodcock. These aspects are important, as we need not only to safeguard our current sport with woodcock but attract more and younger people to it. However, we must pass on to these people not just the skills and wherewithal to find and shoot woodcock, but also an acceptable ethos in relation to woodcock; an appreciation of and a love for woodcock, which is accompanied by the core responsibility to protect this sport for future generations. Later in the book therefore, I will discuss the future for woodcock hunting as I see it through examining the potential threats to it. However, I will also argue that we, the sporting community, have to examine our practices in relation to woodcock.

It is heartening to note as I write this introduction that, following the establishment of the Welsh Woodcock Club/Clwb Cyffylog Cymru in 2005, similar organisations have been set up, namely the National Woodcock Association of Ireland and the Scottish Woodcock Club. These are pro-active hunting and conservation organisations that declare in their constitutions their willingness to take up the political cudgel on behalf of woodcock hunters across the UK and Ireland. Moreover, this momentum has grown under the leadership of my good friend Dr Jean Paul Boidot, ex-President of the Club Nationale de Bécassiers (CNB) in France, who worked tirelessly to form the Federation of National Associations of Woodcock Hunters from the Western Palearctic (FANBPO). This pan-European association has member clubs in France, Italy, Spain, Greece, Switzerland, Wales, Ireland, Scotland, Portugal, Hungary and Belgium.

By early October in any year, my personal countdown has started and the compulsion to 'weather-watch' across Scandinavia and north-west Russia is simply too strong to ignore. My 'moon-gazing' sessions change from simply utter amazement with that essential body towards a focus of another kind. Despite what the cynics claim, I will always connect the full moon with the arrival of woodcock. At the start of October I assume a brief nightly vigil of watching the moon turn through its phases towards full. Not just a huge orb but a beacon for woodcock and woodcock hunters. For, in late September and early October, there are always 'pathfinder woodcock', as the late Colin McKelvie used to describe them, to be found.

My love of hunting woodcock, my thirst for more and more knowledge of them, of their ways, of their habits, was in my estimation only ever matched by that of Colin McKelvie. However, his knowledge of woodcock was, at that time, far superior to mine (which was still developing) and his *Book of the Woodcock* [1st edn 1986] quickly became my bible, as it were, as I read and read and re-read it. Perversely, our friendship began through a spat we engaged in through *Shooting Times* as he defended flight shooting of woodcock at dusk and I challenged and decried the practice. During this exchange of oft-strong views the then editor of *Shooting Times*, Robert Gray, laughingly described us as 'a fine brace of Colins giving it all they're worth in their equal love and obsession for woodcock'. Subsequently, I offered to bury the hatchet and Colin McKelvie, being the kind and generous man he was, graciously accepted my peace offerings. We became firm friends and communicated regularly thereafter. Each season, once the woodcock were in, we communicated on a weekly basis. Colin's knowledge of woodcock was encyclopaedic! He taught me much of what I currently know of woodcock. He also supported my early writings on woodcock in a patient and guiding manner, showing no hostility ever to this 'young Turk' emerging onto the woodcock scene. We never actually met, and I regret that hugely. This book is dedicated to his memory, for it was he and not me who put woodcock firmly on the British and European sportsman's agenda for hunting and conservation.

CHAPTER 1

Woodcock Today

Some dedicated woodcock shooters would sooner give you their credit card number than disclose how well they are doing in terms of numbers shot – let alone the exact venue. There is little exaggeration here! This is the secrecy of tradition and culture. Twenty or thirty years ago the average 'ordinary working man' had little to choose from in relation to quarry species. Myxomatosis had virtually wiped out the rabbit population, and pheasants in many rough shooters' gamebags were particularly rare. The woodcock, however, were seasonal visitors that cared nothing for organised shoots or the ability to pay. They came to the south and west of the British Isles in significant numbers and sprinkled themselves across accessible shooting ground – accessible, that is, to those who knew where to ask and how to ask. Thus, we had the tradition of freely available sport of a quality that most people would give their eye-teeth for. Sadly, to an overwhelming extent, those days are gone forever. Sport with woodcock is now far more difficult to acquire, as access to the land is far more restricted than it was a few decades back. The woodcock, however, are more numerous than ever before. I know this for a fact. Through my 'other' obsession, fly fishing, I have built up a network of 'woodcock obsessives' in both Scotland and Ireland. We talk to each other, you see, before, during and after the season. This is a small example of the extent of some people's interest. We share a love for our sport through our interest and admiration for our quarry.

From the end of October to the end of January, real shooting means going after the woodcock. On average, this means twice a week and sometimes from dawn until dusk. It is the *sport* of it all that entices me time after time. I care barely a jot as to how many I bag: I get my main pleasure from hunting them and flushing them. I find it far more satisfying to flush them in big numbers than to shoot them in big numbers. Like most rough shooters I do, of course, like to shoot well, as that is also an enjoyable part of the process, but the total number flushed,

Gone away!

how many I put up, is equally important to me as it gives me some indication whether all is well with woodcock, or not. I thoroughly enjoy shooting woodcock but, conversely, I also thoroughly enjoy seeing them fly off unharmed.

More than being simply an annual event, this has become almost a pilgrimage: a return, year on year, to those wild, ragged, scrub-covered valleys, cwms and lowlands that I have visited on innumerable occasions since I was a boy. It is also a continuing link with my sporting heritage; the stuff of memories and remembrance. As mentioned in the Introduction, my infection was transmitted to me at a tender age by an uncle who was, as I was to become, a total enthusiast for woodcock shooting. It was he who made sure that, for the rest of my life, the full moon in October would have greater significance than any young mind could have imagined. This association of woodcock migration to the lunar cycle simply acted to enhance the myth and magic that surrounded this annual event. It still does! Late October still finds me moonstruck. I am easy to find in the late evening from mid-October onwards. Inevitably, I am out in the garden viewing the moon, willing it to turn full. I usually have one eye on the weather as well – especially on wind direction. A favourable wind at this time of year would be one from the north or east.

But what of current trends in woodcock numbers? Woodcock are probably the least researched quarry species on the hunter's list. There has been much recent debate, especially within the European Union, as to the woodcock's conservation status. Those on the 'green' side of the debate almost inevitably claim a diminishing number of woodcock across Europe, whilst those on the hunting side of the hedge claim woodcock numbers to be at least stable and even increasing. Of greater concern perhaps is the fact that the woodcock does not lend itself readily to being researched, to be found, let alone quantified. Nevertheless, based upon the flimsiest of evidence, the European Union Draft Management Plan for Woodcock 2006 and 2007 claimed unfavourable conservation status. However, Birdlife International/EBCC (2000) showed that, in the majority of European and Baltic countries with sizeable numbers of breeding woodcock, numbers were, in fact, stable. In fact, an increase in numbers was reported for Denmark, Ireland, Holland and Spain. In France, the monitoring of roding males since 1988 shows the French breeding population to be stable and probably increasing [Ferrand and Gossman 2001]. (Roding is the term attached to the courtship behaviours of male woodcock as they display in an attempt to attract females.) Dr Yves Ferrand, a woodcock hunter and scientist for the Office Nationale de la Chasse et de la Faune Sauvage – the French Game and Wildlife Department – has argued recently that numbers are stable and probably on the increase [Ferrand (article on monitoring French populations) 2008]. His estimations, and those of his colleague Dr François Gossman, are based upon over twenty years of research across France and, also, are gleaned from the joint French–Russian Woodcock Research Project of which he is one of the leading scientists. Without doubt, in relation to European woodcock research, the French are leading the way. In addition to the work undertaken by the statutory game and wildlife department, there are also the extensive activities undertaken by the Club Nationale de Béccassiers (CNB) – the French Woodcock Club. In an average shooting season, through its members' activities, the CNB will process (examine) woodcock wings and trap, net and ring approximately 3,000–5,000 woodcock. This they have been doing for the past twenty years as, very early on, they recognised the absolute need to be able to defend their hunting of woodcock by being able to produce the counter argument via data collection and scientific facts.

The CNB has not only carried out such sterling work in France, but has spread the idea that we need like-minded organisations in all member states. Unfortunately, UK sportsmen have been dragging their heels as, prior to 2005, no such organisations existed in the UK or Ireland. However, in 2005 I successfully persuaded a group of woodcock enthusiasts in south-west Wales to set up the Welsh Woodcock Club (WWC). In 2006 this was followed by the Woodcock Association of Ireland and in 2007 the emergence of a fledgeing Scottish Woodcock Club. These clubs are not simply gatherings of woodcock hunters. They all have conservation objectives and would only support the responsible hunting of woodcock. In 2006, through its membership of the Federation de Associations Nationales des Bécassiers du Palearctique Occidental (FANBPO) – the European Federation of Woodcock Hunting Clubs – the Welsh Woodcock Club was able to warn all of the other UK-based shooting organisations of the existence of the European Union (EU) Draft Management Plan for Woodcock 2006. Moreover, the club was able to respond to the draft plan through working collaboratively with the British Association for Shooting and Conservation (BASC). This, I hope, was a wake-up call to all field sports enthusiasts in the British Isles. We simply cannot ignore the European Union, let alone the influence of the 'greens' and the anti-bloodsports organisations over it. This exercise was repeated in 2007 and again the European Federation of Woodcock Hunting Clubs (FANBPO) responded, as did the WWC. At the time of writing, the issue has not gone away as it is clear that the Director General for Environment has noted the criticisms of his team's robustness in relation to the 'facts' they suggested and the whole process is under review. As surely as God made little woodcock, it will arise again and we must be ready – but what of actual woodcock densities?

In the winter of 2001 I was driving west along the M4 when very suddenly I became aware of a woodcock flying directly towards me in the inside lane. On it came unwaveringly, but I was convinced it would swerve at the last moment. It did not and, in fact, it flew smack into my windscreen. There was an explosion of feathers and it tumbled through the air over the top of my Land Rover and, through my rear view mirror, I saw it bouncing back along the motorway. Was this a sign? Around that time, I had read a piece in *Shooting Times* outlining the British Trust for Ornithology's (BTO) claim that woodcock were in decline and should go on the amber list as a threatened species. What were they talking about? There was no decline in numbers as far as I was concerned. I saw them everywhere, out hunting, flighting past my house at dusk, on the meadows after dark whilst out 'lamping' foxes and – perhaps more importantly as a dedicated woodcock hunter – my records showed no decline but, in fact, an increase in numbers year-on-year since 2000. Most people only count the ones they shoot. I count the ones I see and I count every woodcock flushed on a shooting day and use a clicker to do so. I also count them as they flight out to feed at evening time, at the same locations each week, as do several of my friends at their chosen locations. This gives us a very good idea of how numbers are holding up across our region and elsewhere. On top of all of this assessment, from 2007, members of the Welsh Woodcock Club have been netting, ringing, ageing and counting woodcock feeding on meadows and grassland after dark. Since the year 2000 I have been collating information on woodcock numbers from across the UK and Ireland from other woodcock hunters and gamekeepers. There was – and is to date – no decline in woodcock numbers that I am aware of. In fact, over my shooting lifetime, numbers have increased. This could be shown from the detailed records I have kept since I was a teenager. Testimony to this view is also provided by other lifelong woodcock shooters.

But, what of that M4 woodcock? I did momentarily consider it to be a kamikaze woodcock sent by the Mother of all Woodcock to seek revenge upon me. Quite sensibly for once, I did not stop on the hard shoulder to run back to get it. However, it did spur me to write my first piece on Woodcock for *Shooting Times*. I challenged the notion of decline there and then as I would now. The woodcock is the success story of the quarry list. They are thriving and increasing. Within the last decade we have witnessed some staggering winter populations of woodcock. As we know from the earlier seminal work of Colin McKelvie – *The Book of the Woodcock* [1986] – nine out of every ten woodcock that we encounter in the winter, in the British Isles, are in fact migrants. In the 2005–2006 season I witnessed the largest number of wintering woodcock I have ever experienced. They simply came and came and came. We experienced what Colin McKelvie and I had been waiting for, that is, an exceptional woodcock season with incredible numbers of migrant woodcock resident in the UK and Ireland. Such a migration we had quite vulgarly called the 'large dollop'.

CHAPTER 2

Natural History

What type of bird is the woodcock? Classified by ornithologists as a wader, it is nevertheless a bird of the woodland edge, of marginal land, of upland heather and lowland scrub. This wader is seldom found feeding on the foreshore – except during times of exceedingly cold weather – but, being a nocturnal feeder, is a regular night-time visitor to earthworm-rich pastureland.

The woodcock is commonly described as a sedentary and solitary bird that overwhelmingly enjoys its own company whilst at roost. Whilst the woodcock is a solitary daytime rooster, its nocturnal feeding habits show it to be less concerned about isolation and space as two, three, or more woodcock are often found feeding in close proximity to each other. The blanket of darkness can lull these birds into a sense of false security. For example, the most effective method of netting and ringing woodcock depends upon this blanket of darkness for its success. This method employs two basic items of equipment; a powerful hand-held lamp and a very large, round, landing net borrowed from a salmon fisher. On wet, misty nights especially it is relatively easy to get within netting distance of woodcock. Picked up in the beam of light as they go about busily probing for earthworms they invariably, on a good, dark night, remain almost rooted to the spot. A careful approach and an equally careful netting action is all that is required. However, it is not that easy and does require some practice. Above all, under British Law it can only be done by a British Trust for Ornithology licensed ringer.

It is noticeable, that on the feeding pastures during the hours of darkness, woodcock are more inclined to scuttle about than take flight. On wet and windy nights at least you are in with a good chance. On still, cloudless nights, however, they are up and gone as soon as you enter the field. The glow of self-satisfaction and personal reward, as one holds and rings these wild birds has to be experienced to be fully appreciated. In fact I find the experience of capturing them, handling them, admiring their beauty, ringing and releasing them to be an overtly humbling experience and one which gives me equal satisfaction to that of hunting and subsequently shooting them. There are similarities in both exercises. Predominantly it is a fact that the hunting instinct is to the fore whether one is lamping and catching them or out shooting. Clearly the end result is different, but I have no qualms in harvesting this wild resource. I fully accept the moral responsibility for putting different kinds of meat on my table.

Here, we are dealing with the European or Eurasian woodcock (*Scolopax rusticola*) but worldwide there are eight known types of woodcock to be found. Next to the European woodcock, the American woodcock (*Scolopax minor*) is probably the second best-known type as it is also hunted extensively. In Indonesia, Sumatra and New Guinea resides the dusky woodcock or rufous woodcock (*Scolopax saturata*) and throughout the Far East, through Indonesia to the Philippines, we have the moluccan woodcock (*Scolopax rochussenii*) found only in localised regions. The moluccan woodcock, also known as the Obi woodcock, after the island it inhabits, is the largest of all woodcock and is recorded as being 26% larger that its European cousin the Eurasian woodcock. In comparison therefore, this would put these moluccan woodcock on average somewhere in the region of 16 oz (453 g). This makes it a very sizeable woodcock indeed, but not by any means the largest woodcock species to be recorded. In his book *Snipe and Woodcock* (1903) in the Fin and Feather Series, L. H. de Visme Shaw refers to a W. Yarrel who himself cited an enormous woodcock (*Scolopax rusticola?*) shot in the eighteenth century which weighed 27 oz (765 g). Moreover, soon after this event, one of 24 oz (680 g) was shot. These are remarkably large woodcock. The biggest, at 27 oz (765 g), is only 5 oz (142 g) under 2 lb (0.9 kg) in weight. In comparison, the average weight for a cock pheasant is about 2lb 8 oz (1.13 kg). For his part, de Visme Shaw was convinced that such birds had been shot:

> Evidence as to the accuracy of the recorded weight of these birds is little to be doubted...I have always...found myself compelled to believe that up till a century or so ago there existed in small numbers a distinct species of large woodcock of which the birds mentioned... were members.
>
> de Visme Shaw [1903: 128]

As further 'proof' of their existence, he also suggested that these very large woodcock were common in the eastern counties of England and were known by locals as 'double cock'. For de Visme Shaw these were a distinct sub-species of woodcock. Whether or not this was indeed the case it is now impossible to say. However, it is interesting to note that he himself records examples at 'an ounce or two over the pound', thus being 17 or 18 oz (approximately 480–510 g). These, in themselves, by today's standards, are large birds. In a lifetime of woodcock shooting, having handled thousands and thousands shot by myself and others, I have only ever come across four woodcock weighing more than 16 oz (453 g) and these only marginally so!

From the eight different types of woodcock identified, it is only the European and American woodcock that are truly on the hunted species list. The American woodcock (*Scolopax minor*) is a much smaller bird than its European cousin. For example, it weighs an average of 6–7 oz (170–198 g). Its plumage is similar to that of our European woodcock in that it is russet and brown coloured, but the colouration of the breast feathers is much lighter than its European cousin, ranging from fawn to beige. An altogether dainty bird, it nevertheless resembles the Eurasian woodcock in all other aspects except size. Estimates of population numbers by the United States, Fish and Wildlife Department (2007) were inconclusive. In some States, numbers are stable, while in others numbers appear to be dropping. In the Eastern Region of the USA numbers of displaying woodcock (*Scolopax minor*) declined in 2007 but in the Central Region they remain unchanged. The Department also undertook a 'singing ground survey' of males as they sing during courtship. In both the Eastern and Central Region no significant decline was observed. However, using the same methods in 2008, the Department concluded that 'numbers of displaying woodcock in the Central Region declined 9.2% from 2007…the Eastern Region was unchanged…There was a significant decline in the Central Region'. The Department also estimated that American hunters had harvested approximately 76,000 woodcock in the 2007–2008 season [Cooper et al. 2008]. The main threat to population numbers is seen as habitat loss through urban and agricultural development. It would seem that, in the USA as here in the British Isles and Europe, the changing face of agriculture, the technological advances of agriculture, are having a negative impact on woodcock populations.

However, for the Eurasian/European woodcock the situation appears to be far more secure. Recent research by eminent woodcock scientists here in the UK and in France show the European woodcock population trends to be at worst stable and probably, at best, on the increase. In 2003 Dr Andrew Hoodless of the then Game Conservancy Trust initiated a national survey of breeding woodcock across the UK. In all, 900 woods were surveyed for evidence of roding males. Roding male woodcock were recorded at 416 of the sites, giving a frequency of 44%.

Dr Hoodless' survey results suggested that woodcock were not evenly distributed across the UK. In fact, there was the highest preponderance of woodcock in the south-east of England, with the lowest in Wales. Southern Scotland and the north of England showed higher levels of multiple occupancy. Dr Hoodless concluded from his 2003 study that the breeding population of woodcock in the UK was approximately twice that cited in the British Trust for Ornithology's *New Atlas of Breeding Birds* 1988–1991 [Hoodless 2003]. In addition, it should be noted that, owing to their sedentary and isolationist nature, woodcock do not lend themselves easily to monitoring surveys. Moreover, the number and the location of sites used are problematical. Breeding woodcock are not easily found, let alone seen. At the time of writing, the most recent research on the numbers of resident breeding woodcock in the British Isles by Dr Hoodless of the Game and Wildlife Conservation Trust (GWCT) in March 2009 estimates there to be somewhere in the region of 78,500 or so pairs of potentially breeding woodcock. Prior to this, the British Trust for Ornithology (BTO) had earlier suggested that resident woodcock numbers had declined to somewhere between 5,000 and 12,500 pairs. As previously stated, I never did accept this because of the problematical nature of the survey method. The recent research by Dr Hoodless suggests that the actual breeding population is some ten times higher than previously suggested. However, I would reiterate the fact that woodcock are not easily studied; they do not lend themselves readily to being counted and presented in a statistical manner, because they are most active at dusk and during the night-time. Therefore, whilst Dr Hoodless' revised estimation of breeding pair totals overall is to be welcomed, there may be, in fact, far, far more woodcock than he or I imagine or could hope for! There are still massive tracts of suitable woodcock breeding habitat across the British Isles where nobody goes from one year to the next, let alone at dusk or during the night. Moreover, there are countless isolated places where only stalkers, keepers or forestry workers ever go – and even then they are only infrequent visitors. To my knowledge, no organisation or game shooting body in the British Isles uses or encourages such people to collect information on resident or even migratory woodcock. On this general point, it would also be true of gamekeepers, who are similarly not included in any of the surveys dealt with here. Dr Hoodless' method was based upon counting displaying males at sites across England predominantly. But how many tens or even hundreds of thousands of roding males go unaccounted for in other parts of Scotland, Wales and Ireland, as there is simply no one there to observe them? We also know from previous studies that birds born in these separate regions of the British Isles do, in fact, journey between these regions in the sense that they undertake internal migrations within the British Isles. My gut instinct is, as it was prior to this new research in 2009, that there are far more resident woodcock than the GWCT research suggests.

It occurs to me that one very good method of finding resident woodcock is that employed throughout Canada and the USA of using pointing dogs to locate woodcock on the nest. This practice has quite a long history in the northern states of America. G.A. Ammann of the Michigan Department of Natural Resources, Wildlife Division, produced an information document on 'banding woodcock broods' (ringing the chicks on the nest and the female also, if caught) as far back as 1977. He stressed the absolute need for a rock-steady dog that will sit quietly, after locating the nest and brood, whilst the ringing and data collection activities take place. Wisely, he even advocates the use of a lead by a companion as an additional precaution. The thought of an unruly dog lunging at the brood does not bear thinking about, and safety of the brood must be the primary consideration. Ammann also suggests taking a long-handled net, as the females frequently sit tight and are available to be caught themselves. As for the chicks, it is suggested that once the female bird has flushed they will remain frozen to the spot until the first is captured, whereupon the rest will attempt to disperse [Ammann 1977]. As far as I know, nobody in the UK or Ireland uses this method. In fact I am unaware of anyone these days ringing woodcock chicks. With the right equipment – that is, a very good and steady pointer – and the necessary ringer's authorisation from the British Trust for Ornithology, this is a particularly attractive method of ringing young woodcock which would also give an additional insight into resident breeding populations. Such practice is now widespread throughout North America, having first commenced in Maine in 1937. It could take off here in the UK, and in Ireland and Europe too!

It is undoubtedly the case, as reflected in the literature on woodcock, that most woodcock nests are found by accident, by someone almost walking on them or very near to them. Given the remarkable camouflage a woodcock possesses, the type of cover it nests in and the general terrain, it is nigh on impossible to consider that even the most committed searcher for nesting woodcock is actually going to find, let alone spot, many. However, imagine how much suitable ground and cover an effective pointer could search and eliminate in a day. I suspect that, in those areas where we already know that woodcock are inclined to breed, the number of resident breeders discovered would significantly increase through using this method. The alternative is that we continue making educated guesses and only count roding males.

A very pertinent question here is that of how many receptive females there are in each male woodcock's territory. The current indication is of male activity; it does not and cannot log every male woodcock in even a small locality, let alone across the country, and it tells us absolutely nothing about female woodcock numbers in that locality. They could be more, significantly more, than one would expect. Year after year I receive reports from British gamekeepers notifying me of woodcock nests they have literally stumbled across. I would dearly love to visit these places, accompanied by a suitable pointer, to ascertain exactly what the numbers of woodcock nesting locally actually are. This will be my next project.

Whilst it is notoriously difficult to get people to respond to a survey of any kind, I do think (from experience) that it is possible to set up a network of those people who are particularly interested in woodcock. It should be possible, therefore, to set up a network of gamekeepers and others whose employers would be willing to participate in having the land under their control surveyed by two men and their pointing dog for nesting woodcock.

From the Woodcock Inquiry 1934–35 we can see that, even as a result of predominantly accidental discoveries (and certainly in the complete absence of any structured or co-ordinated assessment), nesting woodcock prior to the 1934–35 Inquiry were, in fact, widespread across the UK and Ireland. It would be useful and scientifically stimulating to revisit some of these places to ascertain whether such breeding activity still occurs. Counting roding males would give some indication of such activity, but a week's nest hunting over a pointer would be far more productive.

Some of the places in Wales cited by W.B. Alexander in 1939 are well known to me. The great estates of Penllegaer and Margam Park are now in Local Authority/Unitary Authority control. However, both were recorded as having breeding woodcock in the early decades of the twentieth century up until the last such report in 1935. Further west, Alexander reported woodcock breeding regularly on the Penrice estate on Gower and his informant claimed them to have done so since time immemorial [Alexander 1939: 24]. I know these places very well and I have no reason not to believe that woodcock breed there to this day. As elsewhere in England, Scotland and Ireland these estates have been broken up and sold off. The only loss relevant to this discussion is that those who were effectively employed as gamekeepers were also full-time observers (and very good and knowledgeable observers, as they are today) of all wildlife. Who now walks such places with one eye open for signs of woodcock flighting or nesting? Very few indeed, I suggest.

I am afraid that overall we have little idea of the true numbers of breeding woodcock. What is required is a multi-method assessment across the UK and Ireland and, of particular importance, one that is preceded by an initiative to prepare the ground by first of all enthusing, organising and training regional volunteers. There are, however, lots and lots of bird watchers and ornithological groups that are out there doing this kind of work. For example, in May 2009 Gwent Bird Watching Group (South Wales) members, via their website, were reporting roding woodcock at Wentwood, Gwent, on the 10th and 21st of that month, with further sightings in June 2009, and other members reported roding woodcock at Ninewells Wood in Gwent again in May 2009. A trawl of the internet would reveal (I know, because in part I have done it), thousands of such sites across the UK, Ireland and Europe, where similar groups record and share their sightings of woodcock amongst other birds. What is really required is for some funding body to sponsor this type of 'desk research' for two or three days to give us an idea of the number of woodcock being sighted in the UK and Ireland. To date, I know of no such scheme having been undertaken. There are far more observers of woodcock out there than our representative sporting bodies appear to appreciate. Yet again, as with gamekeepers, foresters and others, they are not being utilised or sought out.

In France, Dr Yves Ferrand of the French Game and Wildlife Department maintains that woodcock numbers are stable and probably on the increase. It is estimated that a staggering three million woodcock visit France as migrants each winter. The woodcock monitoring programme in France is, in fact, a joint effort between the Office Nationale de la Chasse et de la Sauvage (Game and Wildlife Department) and the Club Nationale de Béccassiers (the French National Woodcock Club). Since 1997 this collaborative project has analysed many thousands of woodcock wings and averages 6,000–10,000 thousand wings per season. This particular exercise allows them to deliver an age ratio of birds shot divided into juvenile or adult. In addition, they also net and ring somewhere in the region of 3,000–5,000 woodcock each winter.

Given that bag returns on woodcock are also mandatory in France, this joint project does deliver very accurate assessments on population trends for the Eurasian woodcock.

On a more localised level, assessments of migrant woodcock can also be usefully undertaken by other methods. On the feeding grounds after dark, using an equation of 'numbers seen per hour's observation', woodcock numbers can be assessed using nothing more scientific than a powerful spotlight. Over time, a record can be amassed showing a ratio of abundance for particular weeks and for months from October through to March when the spring migration will commence. The second method is to find a well-used flight line or crossing point at dusk and to count woodcock flighting on a weekly basis throughout the same period. Again, these records will show, albeit roughly, an abundance ratio in the locality. If sportsmen cannot commit to any of these activities they must, at least, keep good records of woodcock seen and shot during their days in the field. In addition, they can also quite easily age the woodcock shot, a matter dealt with later in this chapter.

The majority of woodcock that visit the UK and Ireland are birds from Norway, Sweden, Finland, the Baltic States, north-west Russia and the Ural Mountains region of Russia, with lesser numbers from Denmark, Holland and France. There are, of course, resident populations of breeding woodcock in both the UK and Ireland. These migratory woodcock can be separated into long-distance migrants that journey over 1,500 miles (2,400-plus km), medium-distance migrants over 900 miles (1,450 km) and short-distance migrants that only shift around 200 miles (320 km) or so. Whilst scientists have some concerns in relation to continued suitable habitat for breeding – especially in Russia, where land use is changing and large tracts of land are becoming neglected – there is no major concern over loss of suitable habitat on the breeding grounds. In fact, the woodcock has been seen to be extending its breeding range into Finnish Lapland during the last few years.

Saari, in his discussion of the spread of woodcock (*Scolopax rusticola*) to Finnish Lapland [2006], notes that woodcock had, in fact, been documented in Lapland, the northernmost region under Finnish jurisdiction, as far back as 1906. However, it is his contention that this presence was underestimated and that throughout the twentieth century and into the present century the population has expanded significantly. Up until the 1950s, woodcock appeared to have only reached the border lands just outside the Arctic Circle. However, from the 1950s onwards, Saari claims that numbers increased significantly. Between 1970 and 1999 the number of woodcock recorded had increased 5.4-fold.

Moreover, he shows that in the early years of this present century, numbers continue to increase. In fact, the number of recorded observations has almost trebled. He also makes the point that, given the terrain and geographical isolation of the Finnish Lapland region, the numbers of observations are extremely limited by the available number of observers. In this respect, numbers of woodcock could be much, much higher. He offers a possible explanation for these increases, year on year since the 1990s and through the early years of the present century, as being climate change.

Referencing the *Finnish Bird Atlas* Saari, [2006] argues that the woodcock's range has been expanding northwards since the 1980s. This is a very significant development for the UK, Irish and possibly, the French woodcock hunter. This geographical expansion of the breeding range must be seen as a positive development that can, potentially, increase the overall number of winter migrants. Moreover, as breeding habitat disappears or diminishes in other regions of the woodcock's historical breeding range, these losses are substituted by this gradual shift northwards. This discussion by Saari is very important as it shows how, in little more than fifty years, climate change can affect breeding behaviour and species distribution. However, it is crucial that we protect and enhance the woodcock's breeding areas across its range in Fennoscandia and north-west Russia.

The European woodcock, *Scolopax rusticola*, is a fantastically camouflaged bird. The browns, blacks and russets of its plumage blend perfectly with its surroundings. On its daytime roost the woodcock is almost impossible to spot and both hunter and dog often walk past or over it. Often, the first indication you get is as it erupts from the ground after you have passed. To describe the woodcock as a brown bird simply does not do any justice to its exquisite markings. The pencil-like line drawings of its plumage are indeed a source of beauty.

The European/Eurasian woodcock is not a big bird as such. Standing 8 inches (20 cm) tall and weighing on average 12 oz (340 g) it is at the small end of the European game bird range. It appears to be quite stocky, with short legs. However, it has some unusual distinguishing attributes. For example, its dome-shaped head holds the very large, liquid eyes typical of a nocturnal feeder and flyer. These big eyes are located back on the head, almost behind it, and give the woodcock 360 degrees of vision. The retina of its eye is such that it provides day and night vision. In front and below the eyes we find the woodcock's ears and again they are highly developed sensory, auditory features. These ears are protected by a covering of feathers. Its long bill is specifically designed for probing to find its favourite food, the earthworm. This tactile bill acts, in fact, like pliers to secure and withdraw its prey from the ground. It is usually 2.5–3.15 inches (65 to 80 mm) long and the upper mandible is flexible enough to be articulated so that prey is secured in a vice-like grip, against the rigid lower mandible. Thus, the woodcock's bill is a very well designed, efficient tool. It is also incredibly sensitive and is a mass of nerve endings. It not only serves to catch and secure earthworms and larvae; it is also used as a sensory tool to detect the movements and vibrations of prey in the immediate area. It is often possible to see where woodcock have been actively searching for food by recognising the probe marks they leave behind. These are easiest to find in old cow pats. Once seen and recognised they are never forgotten and another hunting skill is acquired.

The woodcock's food is almost exclusively 'animal' although some grass seeds have been found in some birds. In addition to earthworms, woodcock also consume the larvae of insects, earwigs and other 'upper layer' grubs. However, it is calculated that earthworms make up over 50% of its diet and deliver in excess of 80% of its energy requirement. The availability of earthworms is therefore a determinant of where woodcock are found, especially during the winter months when production and conservation of energy is at a premium.

Surprising, given the incredible natural engineering that has gone into a normal woodcock's bill, there are frequently examples shot of short-billed woodcock. As mentioned earlier, a normal woodcock's bill is in the region of 2.5–3.15 inches (65–80 mm) in length. For most sportsmen, a short-billed woodcock is any example in which the bill, measured from the rear edge of the nostril aperture to its tip, is less than 2 inches (50 mm). From the records we can see that short-billed woodcock were shot throughout the twentieth century and continue to be shot in this century.

Scientists have shown that these are not a sub-species of *Scolopax rusticola* but simply birds with a particular mutation. In the first instance, Dante Fraguglione [1979] a French woodcock expert, focused the European hunter's attention on short-bills, but in the UK it was not until the publication of Colin McKelvie's *The Book of the Woodcock* [1986] that the attention of sportsmen in the British Isles was really drawn to the fact that short-bills existed and were of interest to enthusiasts like McKelvie. Although the first reported example in the British Isles was in 1972, it is subsequent to the publication of McKelvie's book that there have been numerous further reports. These short-bills have varied from the shortest reported – a bill of just over 1.1 inches

Woodcock Fieldcraft and Quarry

Short-bill at just over 1.75 inches (45 mm). Usual bill length is 2.5 inches+ (60mm+). *(Paul Leyshon)*

(28 mm) – to what is regarded as the 'starting point', as it were, at 2 inches (50 mm).

Fraguglione collected a list of 134 short-billed woodcock from all over Europe and remarked that the majority had bill lengths in the range of 1.38–1.77 inches (35–45 mm). However, as mentioned, in the UK and Ireland it was Colin McKelvie who alerted sportsman to these abnormalities and urged them thereafter to report such occurrences. As far as I can ascertain, up until the date of publication of his book, McKelvie had amassed a list of over 130 short-billed woodcock from across the UK and Ireland. The shortest of these was a cock shot in Cornwall in the 1981–1982 season, which had a bill of just over 1.1 inches (i.e. 29 mm). It should be noted that McKelvie's method was to measure from the tip of the bill, the upper mandible that is, to the rear edge of the bird's nostril opening.

For McKelvie, the evidence he collected at that time was starting to suggest a higher preponderance of short-billed woodcock wintering in northern quarters of the British Isles. He cites the example of that well-known woodcock wintering location, Islay in the Inner Hebrides. It is known that densities of woodcock are higher on Islay than probably anywhere else in the British Isles. In the 1985–1986 shooting season on Islay, across fifty-seven organised shooting days, 133 woodcock were shot, of which 20 were short-bills [McKelvie 1986: 191–193]. This is a remarkably high number of short-bills to be shot in a very localised area. Importantly, McKelvie cites the example of seven short-bills shot on the

Short-billed woodcock with a bill length of 1.75 inches (45 mm), shot by Paul Leyshon in November 2004. The upper bird has a normal length bill of 2.66 inches (68 mm). *(Paul Leyshon)*

same day near Sallen in France. For, I believe, there is a tendency for these short-bills to arrive in small groups. This is impossible to prove, of course, but the examples given and my own experiences suggest that this is more than a coincidence. In early January 2007, I examined the first short-bill ever to be reported to me from Carmarthenshire in West Wales. Within a week, another had been shot approximately a mile from the site of the first shooting. On 5th January 2007 I shot my first ever short-bill woodcock at just under 2 inches, i.e. 1.85 inches (47 mm). On the last day of the season I shot another at 1.95 inches (50 mm). I have shot this place for over forty years and had never come across a short-bill anywhere within the locality before that January, when two turned up in three weeks.

Colin McKelvie's instincts directed him towards Finland as the likely source of these short-bills [McKelvie 1986: 185–195]. As he pointed out, woodcock from Finland spread far more widely across Europe, as winter migrants, than birds from other breeding regions do. To date, short-bills have been reported from every nation state across the European Union and from Russia and Finland. This led McKelvie to suggest that the incidence of short-billed woodcock was increasing. Since first reading McKelvie's seminal work on woodcock in 1986 I have measured every bill of every woodcock that I have handled. I have also encouraged friends, acquaintances and readers of my articles to do likewise. To date, in that twenty-two year period I have only come across five such examples, ranging from 1.85 inches (47 mm) to a fraction under 2 inches (50 mm). However, further weight to the theory that short-bills are migrating in groups was added in the 2008–2009 shooting season. During the period 1st November to 8th December 2008, Herbie Lyn from County Down in Northern Ireland examined thirty-two woodcock shot by him and friends. Of these thirty-two birds, twenty-six were short-bills. Unfortunately, other than recording the fact that those woodcock were most definitely short-bills, no exact measurements were taken.

Reproduction

Mating time is a major opportunity to view and assess local woodcock numbers. Courtship usually occurs just before dawn and in the evening at the onset of dusk. As explained previously, in the UK and Ireland the courtship display by the male woodcock is known as 'roding'. The males fly above the level of the trees, in clearings or at the edge of the wood, in a large circular or triangular track, calling and displaying to attract any female woodcock in the vicinity. During this courtship display the male birds tend to adopt aggressive behavioural patterns and they have been seen to chase off other male woodcock and even other bird species. As with flight times at dusk on their way out to feed on pastureland, male woodcock are particularly punctual and appear at around the same time each evening and also at dawn. It has also been noticed that they use the same roding territory season after season and one can only assume that this adherence to particular parts of the wood or forest gives them some unseen advantage in relation to optimal courtship territory.

The males are also using this display to mark their territory and are often also vocal in marking out their patch. These calls have been described as 'frog-like croaks' and high- and low-pitched notes by those lucky enough to hear them. Woodcock are not the silent birds that many people think they are. One November night in 2007, participating in my regular winter evening's pastime of counting woodcock flighting at dusk, I clocked up another first for me in relation to woodcock behaviour. I had already seen five woodcock winging their way down the clearing towards me when number six appeared, heading straight for me this time. I was hiding behind a small alder tree and the bird did not spot me until it was almost directly overhead. It saw me at the last moment, panicked, and was frantically treading air not more than 15 ft (4.6 m) up when it let out an alarm call. I had, until that time, never heard anything like it, but was overjoyed to do so. I found it hard to describe in words exactly what it sounded like until subsequently I was contacted by a Head Keeper in the South of England, who had experienced a similar event. Head Keeper Michael Appleby, accompanied by George, one of his shooting team, was walking along a ride when he saw a woodcock flying towards them. For whatever reason, it only appeared to see them at the last moment and made a loud 'peeping' noise as it veered around them. I am fascinated by these examples for two main reasons. First, in a lifetime's woodcock hunting, I have never heard a single flushed woodcock utter any alarm call. Not one of the countless thousands that my dogs have flushed has uttered a squeak. One could assume that if ever a woodcock were to utter an alarm call it would be in those circumstances of close proximity to the hunter and especially the dog. Sometimes, woodcock sit so tight they get up within inches of the dog's nose but the only sound one hears is the thrashing of the wings. Second, in my example the time was just before dusk, but in Head Keeper Appleby's it was in broad daylight. Both are surprising as the woodcock possesses such effective eyesight both in the dark and in the daylight.

Normally, the main reproductive period for woodcock is March to April. After mating, the male bird plays no further part in the reproductive process. For her part, the female woodcock lays three or four eggs in a shallow nest made of dry leaves at the forest edge or at the side of a clearing, but always in close proximity to potentially good feeding areas. The eggs are grey to buff in colour with blotches of brown and, as such, are equally as well camouflaged as the bird itself. W.B. Alexander [1939] identified the most popular habitats for nesting woodcock as being birch wood or scrub, followed by deciduous oak woods, with an undergrowth of bramble, with mixed deciduous woodland in third place. However, he also noted that woodcock nests had been found in all manner of sites, including larch woods, rhododendron bushes, gorse, hedges, osier beds and garden shrubberies.

Incubation normally takes 20–23 days and the chicks, when born, weigh a mere 0.6 oz (17 g). They quickly leave the nest, led away by the female woodcock. Quite remarkably, they fledge at 4–5 weeks and by that time weigh almost as much as the mother bird. At this time they fly the nest. Up until this time they are safeguarded by their exquisite camouflage and the dutiful diligence of the mother bird. There is so much testimony to the fact that the mother bird carries her young when in danger that this should now be an accepted trait of woodcock behaviour. There is so much evidence, so many witnesses to this act, that it is time we accepted it as fact. In his report on the Woodcock Inquiry 1934–35, W.B. Alexander provided numerous accounts of woodcock being seen to carry their young. Question 13 of that survey asked respondents: 'Have you ever seen parents carrying their young? If so, describe how they do it, under what circumstances and for what apparent purpose, and any other points that may be of interest' [Alexander 1939: 50]. In excess of 300 respondents replied to that particular set of questions and 150 claimed to have witnessed such an act. Many of these witnesses were gamekeepers familiar with the ways of the countryside and are usually considered as very good observers of wildlife. Many of the other witnesses were accompanied by gamekeepers. Interestingly, ninety-seven of these respondents suggested that the chicks were carried between the female bird's legs or tucked between the legs and the breast; thirty-eight suggested they were carried in the feet or claws.

Alexander cites identical testimony from other sources in the British Isles, from Scandinavia, India and North America (of *Scolopax minor*, the American woodcock). Amazingly so, and strengthening the evidence, some of these respondents, with their witnesses, reported chicks being dropped by adults whilst in flight, thus suggesting categorically that they were being carried. One would have to be an extreme example of a conspiracy theorist to suspect a global plot in place whereby the locus of interest was to deceive others that woodcock from three continents were capable of carrying their young. Such reports are still forthcoming. Robert Pownall reported to me that, on 7th June 2009, whilst making their way through a wood, several members of a party of dog handlers, participating in a simulated walk-up as a part of the UK Kennel Club working test for spaniels at Chatsworth House Park, flushed a woodcock which was clearly seen by several of them to be carrying one of its chicks. The woodcock was seen to rise from cover and carry its youngster for at least fifty yards. Later, as the manoeuvre was reversed, the same bird, it was thought, carried out exactly the same act and carried its youngster back to the original patch of cover.

I suggest there is little doubt that this intriguing bird can, and does in fact, carry its young when called upon to do so during times of perceived threat, or in order to reach more productive feeding areas.

The sexing of woodcock is not a straightforward task. Whilst it is generally the case that female woodcock are usually larger than males, this is no definitive test. Moreover, unlike other game birds, there is no plumage or colouration distinction between cock and hen birds; both have, normally, identical colouration and patterning. Woodcock can only really be sexed via dissection to expose either the ovaries (female) or testes (male). This, in itself, is not a difficult operation: with the woodcock on its back with its breast uppermost a small, delicate incision in the groin of the right leg will reveal the ovaries or the testes. However,

More white than russet, shot in Brittany. (Dr Jean Paul Boidot)

this is probably best shown rather than described. Also, I am advised that this is best done on the day the bird is shot and certainly within twenty-four hours as, thereafter, it becomes impossible to distinguish between male and female.

Whilst slight colour variations to the normal browns, blacks and buffs of a woodcock's plumage are normally found, there are also extreme variations in colouration that appear from time to time. These variations range from all white, to magpie black and white, to black, to what the French term 'Isabella' (which is light brown with no black markings at all) through to ginger. In between, woodcock with white wings or some white primaries turn up each season. The crucial question here is: 'How do these extreme variations manage to survive given the nature of their habitat and absolute need to remain undetected? Whilst a 'normal' woodcock is very difficult for even a predator to spot, one would imagine that an all-white woodcock would stand out in the leaf litter and be easily spotted. (Tawny owls, domestic and feral cats, and foxes are the woodcock's main predators.)

A very light-coloured woodcock, termed 'pastel' by the French.
(Dr Jean Paul Boidot)

A totally white woodcock shot in France. They are rare but turn up on occasion.
(Dr Jean Paul Boidot)

White-winged woodcock. *(Dr Jean Paul Boidot)*

A 'magpie' woodcock – very rare but completely authentic.
(Dr Jean Paul Boidot)

An 'Isabella' woodcock. *(Dr Jean Paul Boidot)*

Known as a 'partial Isabella' by the French.
(Dr Jean Paul Boidot)

Almost black: shot in the Jura Mountains region of France. *(Dr Jean Paul Boidot)*

Woodcock Fieldcraft and Quarry

The woodcock has often been described, quite loosely sometimes, as an enigmatic bird. However, it has become less of riddle with the advance of science. Currently, two separate areas of interest pertaining to the woodcock's existence and habits are under examination. First, in folklore the woodcock was referred to as the 'surgeon bird' in that it was claimed that the bird tended to its own injuries, dressed its wounds. Birds have frequently been found with 'plaster cast-like' dressings applied to their legs. These have been seen to be constructed of feathers from the bird itself mixed with grass, moss and mud. Cynics have always claimed that such appendages became accidentally attached to the birds' wounds or legs. It is surprising, however, that until comparatively recently no one appeared to examine them in detail. There is no historical evidence that I can find of any autopsy taking place to establish exactly what lay below the cast. However, in recent years, Dr Jean Paul Boidot of the French Woodcock Club, a retired veterinary surgeon, has closely examined numerous woodcock carrying mud plaster casts and has shown conclusively that, beneath the mud and materials, there are signs of

The 'surgeon bird'. This bird had a mud and feather 'cast' with no articulation at all in an otherwise well-mended leg.

Natural History

A mud cast on one leg, indicating deliberate dressing of injuries. *(Dr Jean Paul Boidot)*

A very well-constructed bandage of feathers. *(Dr Magot)*

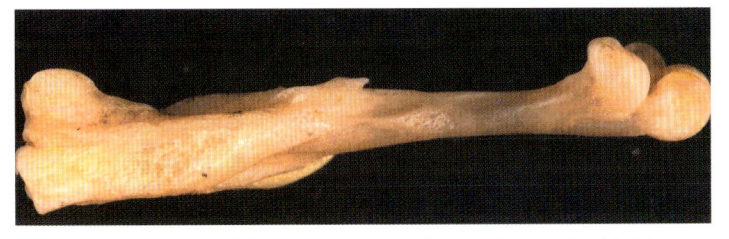

A well-mended leg injury, but not perfectly so. *(Dr Jean Paul Boidot)*

Woodcock Fieldcraft and Quarry

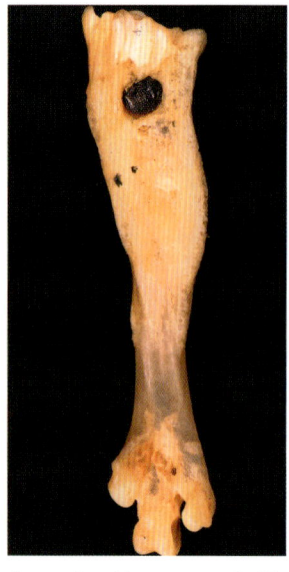

A woodcock's metatarsal with an embedded pellet.
(Dr Jean Paul Boidot)

Mud cast over a leg injury which, when X-rayed, revealed a pellet embedded in bone.
(Dr Jean Paul Boidot)

A dreadful injury. The right foot was at a right angle to the leg and only one toe remained.

injury and physical trauma. It is common practice for Dr Boidot to X-ray such birds before removing the plaster cast to show the injuries beneath and pellets embedded in the bones. In the photographs on page 40 we can clearly see the cast made of feathers and mud and, when cleared away, a shotgun pellet embedded in the leg bone. The photograph on page 40 shows a one-legged woodcock where the missing leg's remaining stump looks to have been surgically removed. I can vouch for the fact that it was not, as I shot it myself. However, the injury was perfectly healed, the bird flew well and was in good condition.

In Canada, Michael Gelinas, another woodcock enthusiast, is also very interested in such injuries. He has a vast collection of photographs of similar occurrences. This collected evidence from both sides of the Atlantic puts beyond doubt the fact that woodcock, both *Scolopax rusticola* and its American cousin *Scolopax minor* are deliberately, purposefully, dressing their injuries and wounds and that a high rate of recovery ensues. It is fantastic that they do so as, fundamentally, the only appendage they have to do it with is that fantastic pliant and sensitive bill of theirs. In fact, the great woodcock man himself pondered as to whether it was possibly true:

> Can it be that woodcock will deliberately mix a combination of mud, leaf fragments, grass and its own feathers to place around the wound?...yet another woodcock mystery.
>
> [McKelvie 1986: 200]

Sadly, Colin McKelvie was never to know that it is, indeed, the case that woodcock tend their own wounds as he very much suspected. Modern science has shown this to be the case. In his study of 'Bone Injuries and Skeletal Abnormalities in Woodcock' [1989] Berlich examined seventy-eight woodcock, fifteen of which showed repaired fractures and/or deformities. Most of these factures and healed injuries occurred in the distal parts of the birds, in the legs and feet, with fewer examples in the sternum and scapula. Berlich confirmed that, at the time of shooting, all were in good physical condition and had flown well.

The hunter can make a valuable contribution to the study of woodcock through the simple process of ageing each bird shot. This we can all do quite easily by examining the different groups of feathers to be found on the upper wing, with reference to the guidelines below. Ageing woodcock by examining their wing feathers can give us a good indication of how productive the previous reproduction cycle was, as it enables us to differentiate those birds shot or netted into adults or juveniles. In a general sense, the higher the ratio of juveniles to adults, the better the indications of successful reproduction the previous spring.

Using the following sequence of instructions, one needs to familiarise oneself with the feathers on the upper wing. On the upper wing (see diagram) we find:
- Primary feathers, the long flight feathers numbered 1–10.
- Secondary feathers, the large feather in line with the primaries following on to the inside of the wing.
- Primary coverts; these are the feathers which overlap the tops of the primary feathers.
- Greater coverts, which overlap the tops of each secondary feather.
- Alula, the feathers which overlap the primary coverts.

IDENTIFICATION AND WING FEATHER COUNT

UPPERWING COVERTS (= FROM OUTER OR *UPPER* WING)

- Primary coverts (1-10)
- Alula (1-3)
- Greater coverts (1-16)
- Reduced primary 11
- Primaries (10 to 1)
- Secondaries (1 to 10)
- Tertials

Reproduced with the agreement of the Club Nationale de Béccasiers and the OMPO, France.

Natural History

Adult primary feather.

Juvenile primary feather.

With an adult woodcock, the very tips of the primary feathers are crisp, clean-edged and show no sign of wear as they are new feathers produced by that year's moulting. For the juvenile woodcock, the tips of the primary feathers are distinctly worn, ragged and in extreme cases appear 'moth-eaten'. Juvenile woodcock, in their first winter, still have the feathers they fledged with the preceding spring. By the time we encounter them in the following autumn/winter these feathers have become particularly worn. Juvenile woodcock do not moult in their first year.

Close-up of adult primary feather tip.

Close-up of juvenile primary feather tip.

Adult primary covert.

Juvenile primary covert.

The tip of an adult primary covert feather is quite broad and is characterised by a pale band in the light-buff to white range. Conversely, the tip of the juvenile's feather is narrower and the tip colouration is a continuation of that of the covert feather itself in the light-brown to dark-brown range.

Adult greater covert.

Juvenile greater covert.

* All pictures in this sequence of ageing Copyright Ray Lockyer.

The adult greater covert has a well-defined pattern of light brown interspersed with darker bands. More significantly, it is long and wide with well-developed down. In contrast, the juvenile greater covert has a far less distinct pattern to it and is short and thin, with far less down.

As with most tasks, lots of practice and familiarity lead to more effective analysis. Quite quickly, one can dispense with the pictorial guide and trust one's skills. The key difference lies in the tips of the primary feathers, the outermost three of which really do enable one to distinguish between adult and juvenile. For most people's purposes this will suffice.

CHAPTER 3

Migration

It is a well-documented fact that the majority of woodcock encountered by the hunter in the British Isles, in late October through to March, are migrants. In fact, as noted elsewhere in this book, Colin McKelvie claimed the ratio of migrants to home-bred birds to be as high as 9:1. The main bodies of migrating woodcock come to the UK, Ireland and north-west France predominantly from Scandinavia and north-west Russia. Birds from other parts of Europe and the Ural Mountains of eastern Russia also migrate to these parts.

Dr Andrew Hoodless of the Game and Wildlife Conservation Trust (GWCT), formerly known as the Game Conservancy Trust (GCT), is clearly our most published and eminent woodcock scientist and currently nobody in the British Isles has ringed as many woodcock as Dr Hoodless. Recently, he has been perfecting the routine of using isotope analysis of feather fibres to pinpoint a woodcock's region of origin. Using an isotope map of north-west Europe, Scandinavia and north-west Russia which illustrates the location of particular trace elements such as hydrogen, carbon and nitrogen (which are transferred into the birds' feather fibres on the nesting grounds), scientists can pinpoint with great accuracy the region of birth of migratory woodcock. Adding this work to the numerous ringing programmes across various countries of Europe, including Scandinavia, Finland and Russia – with sadly little being done in the British Isles – we see that modern science has demystified further aspects of this wonderful bird's life.

However, earlier work at the turn of the twentieth century was surprisingly accurate in its identification of woodcock migration routes. In the 1880s, R.M. Barrington provided very accurate details on woodcock migration patterns to Ireland with only the most rudimentary of resources available to him. Using lighthouse keepers to report woodcock movements – they are frequently attracted to the light emitted, like moths to a flame – Barrington suggested that the main migration into what is now the Irish Republic was from the north of Ireland, since the lighthouse keepers from the northern and north-western lighthouses consistently reported more woodcock than their counterparts across the rest of Ireland on the east and south coasts. In addition, he also claimed that the earliest sightings of woodcock came from the north and, in turn, from the west-coast lighthouses. Richard J. Ussher [1903] drew upon Barrington's survey to conclude that the main migration of woodcock into Ireland came from the direction of Scotland:

> ...it is clear that the flights of woodcock first strike Inishtrahull, the most northerly isle of Ireland...then west Donegal stations [lighthouse stations] follow in point of time.'
>
> [Ussher 1903: 256]

Ussher was of the opinion that woodcock from Scandinavia used Scotland as a resting and jump-off point before crossing over to the northern parts of Ireland. (And, in fact, that woodcock which nested and bred in Scotland also migrated to Ireland.) On reaching the northern coast of Ireland, some would keep to the Antrim coastline and make their way down the eastern side of the country. However, it was Ussher's view that the overwhelming majority took a westward track and proceeded via Donegal down the west coast of what is now the Republic of Ireland. He acknowledged that woodcock did arrive by easterly and south-easterly routes but he thought this to be a less significant migration in terms of total numbers:

> If the majority of these birds that visit Ireland came direct from England and Wales the eastern and southern sides of Ireland would be the most famous for them and they would be reported there earlier in the season. On the contrary, it is the Donegal coast alone that affords notices of woodcocks [sic] in September, but on the south-east coast they are later than on any other.
>
> [Ussher 1903: 258]

Most of what Ussher suspected had, in fact, been suggested by the great Irish naturalist W. Thompson in the mid-1800s. Thompson had been convinced that the main migration points to Ireland were from the north. Time has proved both Ussher and Thompson to be correct. However, Ussher managed to miss the significance – quite understandably so, given the migration data available to him at that time – of the reported late arrival of woodcock on the east coast of Ireland in relation to their possible starting point. Elsewhere in this chapter I have drawn attention to the southern migration route of woodcock into the western fringes of the British Isles across the south-west of England and south-west Wales, by birds which predominantly originate in north-west Russia and the Ural Mountains region of eastern Russia. These are, of course, long-distance travellers and, amongst woodcock migrants, travel the furthest to reach their wintering grounds in south-west Wales and the eastern Irish counties and regions of Waterford, Wexford, the Wicklow Mountains area and the Dublin region. In a way similar to the woodcock on the northern migration route that use Scotland as a stop-over, these birds use the south-west of the British Isles as resting areas and eventually as jump-off points to the east coast of Ireland.

The European woodcock is, I feel, an underestimated traveller of the skies. This relatively small bird, with an optimum migration weight of somewhere between 13 and 14 oz (382–396 g), covers quite some distance to reach its wintering grounds and endures often dreadfully hostile weather conditions to do so. For example, a woodcock born in the Moscow district of north-west Russia would have to fly approximately 1,760 miles (2,830 km) to reach the outer fringes of Pembrokeshire in West Wales (British Isles). Many of these birds would push on, further westward, to the west coast of Ireland. Woodcock ringed in the Moscow and Leningrad districts have been recovered in County Tipperary, County Clare and County Mayo. This adds several hundred miles to an already long-distance migration. Why do so? Why not just reach Pembrokeshire, with its abundance of roosting cover, its predominant dairy farming which produces an abundance of feeding grounds, and simply stay there? What impulse is it that drives the woodcock even further west and forces them to negotiate yet another sea crossing, as if the Baltic Sea, then the English Channel or the North Sea were not enough? What is it that compels some woodcock who find their way to the Iberian Peninsula in south-west Europe to then undertake another journey, across 800 miles (1,290 km) of open sea, to the Azores? Even more perplexing is the fact that the indigenous woodcock of the Azores, the resident breeding population, themselves undertake the reverse journey to the Iberian Peninsula! There are also resident breeding populations on Madeira and the Canary Islands [Snow and Perrins 1998].

Even more staggering is the fact that both the European woodcock *(Scolopax rusticola)* and its smaller cousin the American woodcock *(Scolopax minor)* have migrated across the north Atlantic. On 28 October 2006 a French hunter, Monsieur Jean Brosset, shot an American woodcock at Sorges-en-Perigord in the Dordogne region in France. This juvenile bird was subsequently subjected to a post-mortem examination which ruled out any suspicion that it had been deep-frozen and imported into France. This bird was accepted as true migrant, that had made its own way to France, by the French Aviafaunal Committee and also by the French Rarities Committee [Ferrand et al., Ornithos 15–2: 128–131, 2008]. What makes this feat even more remarkable than just the distance covered, is that the American woodcock *(Scolopax minor)* weighs a mere 4.4–8.5 oz (125–240 g). It is primarily a bird of the eastern seaboard of North America. The route this diminutive bird took to reach the Dordogne is almost unimaginable. It is also significant that it was shot very early in the autumn of 2006, in October, when European woodcock *(Scolopax rusticola)* across Scandinavia and north-west Russia are only just beginning to migrate. However, they too have crossed the great Atlantic pond and have turned up infrequently since 1935 when one was shot by a Mr G.F. Dixon in Cleveland, Ohio.

As regards the British Isles, the majority of our winter migrants are from Scandinavia, the Baltic States and north-west Russia. They do, however, come from further away – as mentioned earlier, woodcock ringed in the Ural Mountains region have been recovered in Ireland. It would appear that woodcock from this region of Russia have two main migration routes. Those from European Russia (including some from the Ural Mountains) migrate west and north-west to France, Portugal, Spain and the British Isles. Others from the Ural Mountains range fly in a generally southerly direction to Iraq, Iran, Israel and south-westwards to Greece, Albania and North Africa.

Migration normally occurs at night, but sometimes also in the day. The first to depart are usually the juveniles and the female adult birds. Migration from north-west Russia usually commences in the last week or so in September and in the Scandinavian countries of Finland, Sweden and Norway around about the first ten days of October. In my region of the UK, the very first sizeable numbers of 'pathfinder' woodcock arrive on or around 23rd October year after year. However, in some years woodcock migration is much earlier and in other years much later than this. I share the conviction that climatic change is having an adverse effect on woodcock migration. But how do they find their way to their wintering ground? Is it by accident or design?

Scientists tell us that adult woodcock are returning to wintering sites they have used before. It is believed that even as chicks they develop a 'night sky map' in their heads and that they fly by using the stars as navigation points. In this sense, those localities have, in fact, imprinted upon them. Regarding juvenile birds, we are told that they find their way to various wintering grounds by accident but thereafter return year after year as ringing recoveries show. What is not explained and perhaps cannot be explained is why they choose particular regions as opposed to other more distant localities. However, it is also known that woodcock often migrate in small groups and this, I think, plays a part in where juveniles eventually end up. Yet again, another unanswered question is: Do the female adults lead the juveniles in generally the right direction? We know that geese do this. Is it good enough to simply accept that an overwhelming number of woodcock trip over or end up in France, whilst a lesser number end up in the UK and, even more accidentally so, some end up on Ireland's west coast? We can accept that woodcock, like other avian migrants, use the stars in the night sky to find their way to the over-wintering grounds, but how do they know they have arrived?

We know from recoveries of ringed birds that woodcock have high levels of fidelity to particular regions and, indeed, to much smaller areas. Woodcock ringed on particular pastureland or particular fields have been recaptured in exactly the same spot in the following or subsequent winters. In November 2008, a woodcock that had been caught and ringed in mid-Wales as a part of the Welsh Woodcock Club ringing programme in January 2008 was recaptured on the same field. On Boxing Day 2008 another bird that had been ringed by the Welsh Woodcock Club in January 2008 was shot within half a mile (0.8 km) of the original ringing site. There are also numerous examples of exactly the same occurrence from the Club Nationale de Béccassiers ringing programme in France. Thus we can conclude that woodcock are, in fact, using landmarks not only to find their way but also to confirm the fact that they have arrived. There is no other possible way of them knowing. For example, through ringing programmes, it is known that swallows return not only to the same region but to the same farm and to the very same farm building they nested in, or were born in, the previous year. Many of these swallows undertake an even greater journey than our woodcock as they migrate between the British Isles and Africa. Across the British Isles, members of the Woodcock Broadcast network have been straining their eyes to spot the early arrivals – and with some success, it would appear.

There is, however, much evidence, both scientific and anecdotal, of woodcock migrating in small groups. Lyn and Emma Murley from South Wales (UK) are avid woodcock spotters. Standing at the same spot they have used over the last several years, half an hour before darkness descends, they count woodcock at least twice a week throughout the autumn and winter up until mid-March. Fortunately for those of us interested in woodcock, they also keep immaculate records of date, time, weather patterns and numbers seen. Thus, over the years, they have produced a very interesting and very useful record of numbers of woodcock seen for a given locality throughout the winter. Such data gathering by committed enthusiasts is unfortunately little used, as it largely remains hidden through an absolute absence of any project to gather such evidence. On the evening of 5th October 2006, waiting patiently and hopefully for the woodcock to put in an appearance (as they had only previously seen two that week), they were suddenly amazed to see eleven woodcock, in a group, pass them just a few feet off the ground. This small group migration is, in fact, well known to observers of woodcock.

In their assessment of increasing migration distances amongst many species of waterbirds and waders, Dobrynina and Kharitonov [2006] draw our attention, in particular, to the fact that a 'steady increase in the length of migration is especially well pronounced in the Eurasian woodcock. In this species, the increase is apparent both in terms of latitude and longitude' [Dobrynina and Kharitonov 2006: 584]. The authors show that migration distances had increased from a mean distance of 1,519.5 km (about 944 miles) in the period 1951–1960 to a mean distance of 2,300.9 km (about 1,430 miles) in the period 1981–1990. Moreover, whilst the mean distance of flights is greater on the east to west routes than the north to south routes, both are increasing steadily year on year.

The genetic impulse that compels woodcock born in north-west Russia, the Ural Mountains region and Fennoscandia to migrate west and south also impacts upon woodcock born in the British Isles. They, too, undertake short and significantly longer migrations between the home nations in the British Isles. Such movements are well documented from the late nineteenth and the early twentieth century. In addition, woodcock born in the British Isles have frequently turned up in France, Spain and Portugal. However, Hoodless [2002] claims that a small majority (51%) of British and Irish birds remain within a relatively local or regional distance from their place of birth. For, records show that the small majority are recovered within 6 miles (10 km) and 18 miles (29 km). He does, however, point out that a significant proportion of 'home-bred' birds do in fact undertake longer distance migration up to and in excess of 300 miles (483 km). These can best be described as genetically induced movements and, as Hoodless points out, there is no evidence that they were caused by severe cold spells. He goes on to note that:

> ...longest distance recoveries were mainly of birds from northern Britain which tended to move south or south-west to Ireland, France, Spain, Belgium, Portugal and Denmark...the fact that the majority of these recoveries were made before 1st January is again indicative that the movements were not made in response to inclement weather...A small proportion of British breeders are truly migratory, leaving northern Britain as birds from Fennoscandia and Russia are arriving.
>
> Hoodless [2002: 320].

It is quite possible that these patterns of migration by northern-born woodcock are a genetic inheritance from the time when Scotland was much, much colder during the winter and the need to move south and west was absolutely essential.

Such patterns of movement were noted by Alexander [1939: 65] but he claimed that these were overwhelmingly 'pre-migrations' in a northerly direction. Of these examples cited by Alexander, two are of particular interest. A woodcock ringed at Port Talbot, in South Wales, on 24th April 1928 was recovered at Appleby, Westmorland (Northumberland nowadays) on 9th September 1928 – a journey of approximately 258 miles (415 km). The other was ringed at Temple House, County Sligo, Ireland on 12th May 1914 and was recovered in the Parish of Nesting, on the Shetland Isles, on 7th July 1917. For Alexander, the vast majority of woodcock (85%) are recovered at or near the ringing location, especially if ringed as chicks, whilst a smaller number (15%) were longer distance travellers. Whilst great fidelity is claimed for woodcock in relation to their wintering grounds and breeding grounds, Alexander was able to show that, in subsequent years, the birds turned up at some significant distances from their ringing sites. For example, a bird ringed at Almonds Bank, Perth, Scotland on the 7th May 1925 turned up at Rush, Dublin, Ireland on 6th January 1926; a bird ringed at

Scone, Perth, Scotland on 27th July 1927 turned up at Kenmare, County Kerry, Ireland on 8th January 1930; a bird ringed at Barronscourt, County Tyrone, Northern Ireland in 1906 was recovered at Harrow, Middlesex, England on 9th January 1907 and finally, a woodcock ringed at Abbeyfield, Lancashire in June 1932 was shot at Camrose, Haverfordwest, Pembrokeshire, Wales on 22nd January 1936. It is interesting to note that each of these 'wayward' travellers was recovered in other parts of the UK and Ireland, some hundreds of miles from their original ringing location, late in the shooting season as we now know it (in January in each example given). In each case they were significantly south or west of the ringing site and could not be said, as Alexander suggested elsewhere, to be on a return journey north or east. He did, however, acknowledge the propensity of woodcock to wander across their European range and that, when you most expect them to turn up on or near their place of birth, their original breeding grounds, they turn up elsewhere. Alexander [1939: 81] described the following three birds as exceptions to the case:

1. Ringed at Classiebawn, County Sligo, Ireland in 1919 as a chick this bird turned up at Frederikstad, 50 miles (80 km) south of Oslo, Norway on 20th April 1921.
2. Ringed at Redgorten, Perthshire, Scotland on 6th May 1931, this bird was recovered at Rollag, Numedal, Norway on 13th May 1932.
3. Ringed as a chick at Classiebawn, County Sligo, Ireland on 6th May 1931, this bird was recovered in Midlothian, Scotland on 23rd May 1921.

By the time of year given for recovery in each of these examples, breeding by resident woodcock in the original nesting area or region where these birds were ringed as chicks would have most likely been underway. Therefore, the 'wayward travellers' of the two Norwegian examples were considerably off course by some 300–400 miles (480–645 km) to the east and one can only presume they, too, were there to breed. Over time there has been some discussion that suggested that such examples were the result of British and Irish-born woodcock pairing up with foreign migrants and then accompanying them back to their breeding grounds in Fennoscandia, Finland or Russia. To date, this is practically impossible to prove and may only become possible to show through enhanced and increased use of satellite tracking. However, cost remains an inhibitor for any medium- to large-scale satellite tracking programme.

Landsborough Thompson in his study of the migration patterns of

British and Irish woodcock [1929] draws our attention to the importance of private ringing schemes at the turn of the twentieth century. Some of these schemes are of greater significance than others owing to the fact that more woodcock were ringed over a longer period and better records of recoveries were kept and preserved. The earliest known scheme was initiated by Lord William Percy in 1891 at his Alnwick estate in Northumberland, England. The records shown by Landsborough Thompson [1929: 75] reveal that, out of a total of 375 juvenile birds ringed only fifty-eight were recovered in the eighteen-year period up to 1909. The other significant scheme around this time was undertaken by Colonel W.W. Ashley at Classiebawn, County Sligo, Ireland in 1910. Over the next nineteen years the Classiebawn scheme captured and ringed 658 juvenile woodcock from which ninety-two were recovered. Both schemes recorded birds recovered at or near the place of ringing. In the Alnwick scheme, birds were also recorded as 'recovered elsewhere in northern Great Britain' and 'recovered outside the general area'. Landsborough Thompson notes the 'general area' is defined as Scotland and the north of England. At Classiebawn, recovered woodcock were also listed as 'recovered elsewhere in Ireland' and 'recovered outside of Ireland'. The majority of woodcock in both schemes were recovered 'at or near the site' of ringing, with forty-five recoveries at Alnwick and eighty-three at Classiebawn. Whilst the figures for birds recovered in the general region are not that far apart in both examples, at four for Alnwick and six for Classiebawn, those recovered outside of Great Britain showed greater variance, with nine recorded from Alnwick and four from outside of Ireland recorded from Classiebawn.

Using information produced in the British Birds Survey 1910 and the Aberdeen University Bird Migration Inquiry 1912, Landsborough Thompson was able to show significant autumn movements of woodcock from the north of England to the south and west of Ireland. For instance, he gives many examples of woodcock from the more northern and southern regions of Scotland migrating to Counties Clare, Kerry and Cork in the south-west of Ireland. In fact, County Cork received more birds from Scotland and the north of England than any other Irish county, but birds from Scotland and England did turn up in other Irish regions except the far north-west. These are clearly not local or regional shifts and are, in fact, longer-distance migrations of several hundreds of miles. Some of these woodcock from northern Britain were also recovered in the south-west of England and France but to a far lesser extent. In opposition to Alexander's observations [1939], all of these birds were heading in a south-western or southerly direction.

Based upon his analysis of the two private ringing schemes – Classiebawn and Alnwick – and those of the British Birds Survey 1910 and Aberdeen University's Bird Migration Inquiry 1912, Landsborough Thompson concluded that between 25% and 33% of woodcock born in the north of England and Scotland were indeed migratory. In fact, he argued that, given that some birds migrated to continental Europe (where reporting back was far more difficult to achieve at that time), the above figures for truly migratory woodcock were probably underplayed and thus were a conservative estimate. It was therefore more than possible – and probably remains so – that a much higher percentage of British-born woodcock do in fact migrate considerable distances. (Although they are by no means 'long-distance' migrants they are nevertheless migratory.) However, he was clear that the number of Irish-born birds undertaking such migration was far, far less. He also noted that recoveries from outside the national boundaries of Ireland and England were far higher than recoveries within national boundaries. This led him to conclude that woodcock are either absolutely local in terms of movement or truly migratory. He does, however, support Alexander's 'northerly pre-migration' thesis by pointing out that the records show movements in a northerly direction in the autumn of the bird's first year. He shows such movements from the north of England into northern Scotland and from South Wales to the north of England; a young bird ringed in Glamorgan was recovered in Westmorland (Northumberland) in October of its first year, having travelled 215 miles (346 km) [1929: 82]. While Irish-born birds apparently undertake long-distance migrations far less, they have nevertheless turned up in south-west France and Spain (both Sligo birds) and also in Portugal (a County Galway bird most likely ringed at Ashford Castle).

Such ringing programmes are not only important for the migration patterns they show; they also give an indication of just how long-lived woodcock are. Drawing upon the Classiebawn records, Landsborough Thompson refers to a woodcock ringed as a chick in 1912 which was recovered on the estate in 1924, twelve years later, having killed itself by flying into a barbed wire fence. Also, he refers to a bird ringed as a chick in Kirkcudbrightshire, Scotland, in 1914 at the outbreak of World War I and recovered on 30th November 1926, the year of the General Strike, in Dumfriesshire some few miles from where it had been ringed, but in a Europe changed for ever by war and strife.

In addition to these two major ringing schemes there were other smaller but important schemes which added to our stock of knowledge of woodcock migration. Overwhelmingly, these were located in the west of Ireland at Temple House, County Sligo under Major A.A. Percival; at Hazelwood, County Sligo under Captain P.D. Percival; at Lissadell, County Sligo under Sir Jocelyn Gore-Booth; at Baronscourt, County Tyrone under Lord John Hamilton; at Cong, County Galway under Lord Ardilaun; at Brookeborough, County Fermanagh under Sir Basil Brooke; with one in England, at Swynnerton Park, Staffordshire under Lord Stafford. These ringing programmes were undertaken in the period 1905–1929. It is important to note not only their historical significance in relation to the contribution they made to our knowledge of woodcock, or their significance as examples of shooting estates with enough resources of time, cheap labour and money to focus almost exclusively on woodcock in terms of 'manpower' and habitat, but also to mark that their demise represents a high point to date in ringing activity for woodcock in the UK and Ireland. Sadly, there appears to be little historical evidence of woodcock ringing schemes in Wales other than two mentions in the literature on woodcock of birds ringed at Margam Castle, Port Talbot, South Wales. This is particularly regrettable given the presence of at least three other notable woodcock shooting estates at Penrice, Gower (formerly in Glamorgan), the Penllegaer Estate owned by the Llewellyn family some 10 miles (16 km) north of Swansea and also, the great shooting estate at Stackpole, Pembrokeshire owned by the Cawdor family where, in the 1960s, the then record bag for woodcock was shot. Moreover, this is doubly frustrating as south-west Wales and the Lleyn Peninsula in north Wales have long been regarded as premier woodcock wintering areas and remain so to this day. Records for Penrice go as far back as 1793 when a white woodcock, which had been observed and shot at for three consecutive seasons, was eventually found dead during a severe and prolonged period of cold weather.

Fortunately, there are some exciting current technological developments in relation to monitoring woodcock. A Spanish project entitled '*Scolopax rusticola* without frontiers' commenced in 2006 when a 12 gram satellite transmitter was fitted to a woodcock, subsequently named 'Trasgu', which was captured in Catalonia. This bird was tracked back to north-east Russia having covered a distance of 2,325 miles (3,740 km). In so doing, it took a flight path from Spain which crossed France, Germany, Poland, Belarus and went on into Russia. In 2007 another woodcock, 'Astur', was fitted with a transmitter and it, too, was tracked back to Russia. It followed a similar route to the first bird but ended up in the Ural Mountains region having covered 2,895 miles (4,658 km). Another bird, 'Navarre', tagged in 2007, was to become the long-distance traveller of the Spanish project to date. This female again followed a similar route across France, Germany and Poland but then headed north across Lithuania, Latvia, and Estonia to pass to the north of St. Petersburg. Up until August 2008 this woodcock had travelled back and forth twice, between her breeding grounds and her wintering grounds. In the winter of 2007–2008 she came back to almost the exact spot where she had been captured and tagged with a transmitter in Catalonia. In 2008, she nested within 1¾ miles (2.8 km) of where she had been pinpointed nesting in 2007. In total she had travelled 7,116 miles (11,450 km) [Felix 2009].

The Spanish Woodcock Club, working with an electronics company between 2006 and 2009, managed to reduce the weight of a satellite transmitter from 12 g to 9.5 g (about ⅓ oz) , a significant development for the woodcock, which themselves weigh only some 12 oz (340 g). However, despite the ground-breaking use of satellite tracking devices, the simple ringing of woodcock still has much to offer. A ringing programme is comparatively cheap in terms of equipment required to net and ring woodcock, the rings themselves, and the time one puts in – which, for most people, is a labour of love. On a large scale, such as the 3,000–5,000 woodcock ringed by the collaborative project undertaken by the French Game and Wildlife Department and the French Woodcock Club every winter, it can be a very productive means of mapping woodcock journeys to and from their breeding grounds. Even on a small scale, ringing a few hundred birds each winter is still worthwhile, as the earlier ringing programmes outlined in this chapter show.

We need far more ringing programmes and far more people, trained far more quickly. Moreover, despite the advances of scientific inquiry and methods of observation there have been relatively few recent studies which have significantly advanced our understanding of woodcock migration. The classical studies dealt with here, by the likes of R.M. Barrington [1900], L.H. de Visme Shaw [1903], J. Schenk [1927], A. Landsborough Thompson [1929], W.B. Alexander [1939] and the major contribution of Colin McKelvie [1986] have not really been superseded, although there is, of course, the work by Hirons and Bickford Smith [1983], Hoodless et al. [2000–2009] and Ferrand and Gossman [1990s–2008] all of which has added to our knowledge of the woodcock's general way of life. That said, I do feel that the greatest potential for unpicking the mysteries of woodcock migration and movements when actually on the wintering grounds will lie in satellite tracking as, hopefully, it becomes far more financially viable to do so.

In 2009 Roy Dennis of the Highland Wildlife Restoration Programme undertook a small-scale project in collaboration with the owners of the

Dunlossit Estate on Islay and supported by Head Keeper Donald MacPhee, whereby two woodcock captured on the island of Islay off the west coast of Scotland were satellite tagged. Two of these Islay birds, given the names 'Askaig' and 'Lossit', were tracked from release on 24th February 2009 up until 16th May 2009 and I am indebted to Roy Dennis who agreed that I could re-describe the routes undertaken by both on their journeys back to their breeding grounds. Using satellite tracking in conjunction with the 'Google Earth' internet site, Roy Dennis was able to show and describe the woodcocks' journeys on a regular basis with updates every couple of days.

> On 25th March 2009 woodcock Askaig set out on her migration and left Islay. Quite surprisingly so, this bird headed in a south-easterly direction towards Humberside.
>
> Two days later, by 27th March, she had crossed the North Sea, having flown 470 miles (756 km) to Germany where a signal was picked up from a location near to Wulfsdorf.
>
> Six days later, she was tracked to Oland Island off the south-east coast of Sweden.
>
> Three days later, on 7th April, she had crossed the Baltic Sea and was located in Latvia.
>
> By 10th April, she was in northern Estonia on the coast of the Gulf of Finland.
>
> On 25th April she was tracked flying over the Gulf of Finland heading east-north-east towards Russia.
>
> By 28th April, with what was described as a 'class A signal', Askaig was found to be near Vologda Oblast, 242 miles (390 km) east of St. Petersburg.
>
> By 8th May she was tracked migrating eastwards at evening time.
>
> By 11th May, after further migration, Askaig was located 155 miles (250 km) east of Archangel, which is just about at the northerly limit of *Scolopax rusticola's* breeding range.
>
> A shorter distance was covered on 14th May and she was tracked to an area of land between the Vashka and Mezen rivers. Finally, on 16th May, she appeared to have reached her final destination and this enigmatic traveller was located to the north of the Mezen River, near the village of Smolentz.
>
> [Highland Foundation for Wildlife 2009].

The route described by this bird's journey is simply fantastic as it crossed nine different countries – Scotland, England, Germany, Denmark, Latvia, Estonia, Sweden, Finland and Russia – to reach her breeding area. I am intrigued by the fact that this bird jumped from Germany in a north-easterly direction across the lower Baltic to Sweden. Why take such a contorted route? Was she confused or, more likely, was this an easier or shorter route that my basic geography does not allow me to understand. Nevertheless, it is an absolutely staggering achievement for such a relatively small bird. Having set off from Scotland some three months earlier, by the time she arrived near Archangel she had covered a staggering 2,360 miles (3,800 km).

The other woodcock trapped on Islay and fitted with a satellite transmitter undertook an entirely different but to-be-expected journey from Islay back to its breeding area.

> This particular bird, named 'Lossit' after the nearby farm, was caught and released on 26th February 2009 and for the remainder of February and the first three weeks of March remained on Islay.
>
> On 27th March this bird flew to mainland Scotland and by 25th March was tracked to a location near Glasgow.
>
> By 27th March, Lossit was on the Fintry Hills north-east of Glasgow.
>
> By 30th March Lossit had crossed the North Sea and was located south of Stavanger Airport, Norway having journeyed 425 miles (684 km) from the Fintry Hills to the north-east of Glasgow.
>
> On 4th April, Lossit had moved 96 miles (155 km) and was found to the south-east of the town of Mandal in Norway.
>
> Up until the last recorded location on 16th May 2009 this woodcock had remained in the Mandal area, presumably having reached breeding grounds.
>
> [Highland Foundation for Wildlife 2009].

Overwhelmingly so, from what I have read in a lifetime's interest of woodcock, this just has to be the most exciting, most productive piece of work on woodcock migration to have been undertaken to date. However, the story does not necessarily end with Askaig's and Lossit's arrival at their breeding grounds in north-eastern Russia and southern Norway.

For, it is claimed that the satellite transmitters have an expected working life of at least three years, which means they can be tracked back and forth between Islay and Russia or Norway in subsequent years and it will be interesting to see on what dates they depart, how long it takes to get to their destination and what routes they take. This, however, presumes that they will in fact return to Islay. We already know from previous ringing programmes that one or the other may become one of the 'wayward wanderers' and end up somewhere else in the UK, Ireland or Europe. Even if this were to happen it will still remain an invaluable piece of research in that we can expect, if the birds do survive, a detailed route map of all of their journeys over the next couple of years or so. The greater likelihood, however, is that they will turn up on Islay if they turn up anywhere. This is already a fantastic achievement by Roy Dennis, Head Keeper Donald McPhee and the owners of the Dunlossit Estate!

Despite the advances of ornithological science and monitoring technology, ringing of woodcock is still, as mentioned earlier, probably the most practical and financially achievable method of building a picture of their travels. The advantage of ringing is that it is not confined to establishing in a general sense the region in which they were born, as isotope analysis does, but that it has the potential to show us where they go *in between* initial ringing and final recovery. Ringing is far less expensive than satellite tracking and relatively speaking the rings will last as long as the bird is alive. Clearly, rings do not allow the close tracking of woodcock that is shown in the Dunlossit example, but ringing programmes are eminently more affordable and act to draw in sportsmen and others as they can participate directly in such activities. These facts are largely the reasons why the ringing programmes in France and Wales are so successful and well supported.

Ringing also gives a very good assessment of longevity. For example, in June 2008, the longevity record for a woodcock as set by Euring, the European Bird Ringing Network, was fifteen years and five months. However, a much earlier ringing recovery shows woodcock to be remarkably long-lived. In *The Woodcock in the British Isles* [1939], W.B. Alexander, Director of the Edward Grey Institute of Field Ornithology at Oxford University, states that, on examining recoveries of woodcock ringed in the British Isles, he found that a woodcock ringed at Goathland, Yorkshire on 27th April 1913 was recovered at St Eulalie-en-Born, Landes, France on 16th November 1933. That Woodcock was twenty years old and had travelled at least 900 miles (1,450 km) to southern France. However, the overall distance for all of the journeys undertaken in that twenty-year period will forever remain a mystery.

Ringing of woodcock has already been taking place for the best part of one hundred years. In his *The Book of the Woodcock* [1986] Colin McKelvie cites the example of the Duke of Abercorn who started ringing woodcock on his Baronscourt estate in 1905. L.H. de Visme Shaw et al. [1903] clearly illustrate a long-standing desire by the British Isles and Irish sportsmen to understand the migration patterns of woodcock.

The migration journey that woodcock undertake has always amazed me. The excitement of waiting for them to arrive has not diminished one iota, but what is it that 'triggers' migration? Clearly, there is an overwhelming genetic influence to do so. This impulse, it is thought, is triggered by what the boffins refer to as photoperiod. That is, diminishing hours of daylight transmit a compulsive signal to the birds that it is time to seek out their wintering quarters in north-west Europe. Weather conditions at this time of year, on the breeding grounds of Fennoscandia and north-west Russia, are of particular significance. An early onset of wintry conditions will invariably result in a shift or even a full-blown migration. It is estimated that 90% of the north-west Europe wintering population of migrant woodcock is derived from Fennoscandia and Russia. There are smaller breeding populations in Denmark, Germany,

Dr Yves Ferrand of the French Game Department *(right)* and Pierre Launay (CNB), ringing woodcock in Brittany.

Ringing woodcock in West Wales after dark.

Belgium, France and the Netherlands. However, given the solitary, sedentary, 'out of the way' nature of the woodcock it is very difficult to produce an accurate figure for these breeding stocks. The woodcock born in Russia or Fennoscandia are truly migratory. Cock from these regions winter throughout north-western and southern Europe, in the UK, Ireland, France, Spain and Portugal. However, woodcock from the Ural Mountains region, the great dividing line between Europe and Asia, migrate mainly to Albania, Italy, Greece, Turkey, Iran and Iraq. Migrant woodcock are extremely faithful to their wintering grounds: year after year they visit the same haunts.

Woodcock wintering in Scotland and the north of England largely originate from Norway and Sweden. In contrast, the majority of birds wintering in the south-west of England and Wales come from Finland, north-west Russia, the Ural Mountains and the Baltic States. Ireland, on the other hand, is thought to receive its woodcock from throughout the northern European breeding range. Colin McKelvie once told me that he was convinced that some of these birds, destined for Northern Ireland, Sligo, Mayo and Donegal, take a circular route around the top of Scotland. The weather, however, can influence and mix this all up as birds are forced to deviate and shift to counteract inclement weather conditions. I once calculated that a woodcock, hatched near Moscow, flying in a straight line to Cardiff, would need to cover 1,673 miles (2,692 km). Absolutely staggering! There are, of course, resting points along the way but this is nevertheless an epic journey for a relatively small migrant that flies rather than glides. By my calculations the shortest crossing would probably be Stavanger in Norway to Aberdeen in Scotland at 314 miles (505 km) across open sea. More often that not, thankfully, the forces of nature work with our migrant woodcock. Historically, throughout the last century, there were frequent reports of numbers of woodcock littered across the North Sea having failed to battle their way through adverse south and south-westerly storms. However, since the advent of North Sea Oil and Gas we have had remarkable reports of woodcock using the oil and gas rigs as resting places during migration. This was documented for me by my friend and correspondent Chris Trewhitt who, working on a gas rig on 12th November 2006, 22 miles (35 km) offshore from Scarborough, came across three woodcock resting on the platform, sheltering from a north-westerly gale. This tale almost beggars belief given the levels of illumination which are standard to these rigs and the burning-off of excess gas via flames that shoot hundreds of feet into the air – except that such occurrences have been widely reported across the last three decades. Imagine how desperate for rest these birds were that they could overcome their instincts not to land in such a place. Doing so runs counter to all of their instincts and is surely akin to flying into the bowels of hell.

The North Sea Bird Club was set up in 1979 and emerged from a natural history group set up by one of British Petroleum's (BP's) operational Directors, Stan Howe. He managed to persuade the likes of BP, Chevron, Conco Mobil, Occidental, Phillips and Shell to sponsor the setting up of an industry-wide Bird Club to report and record all sightings of birds and other wildlife sighted in the North Sea. Over time, this grew to encompass observers on offshore production platforms, rigs, ships, fishing vessels and survey vessels. At one time the Bird Club had over 670 observers plying their hobby offshore. Moreover, the area covered by these volunteer observers expanded to include the English Channel, the Irish Sea, the Atlantic Approaches, the areas to the west of Shetland and the Norwegian sector. Since the club's initiation there have been thousands and thousands of reports of all manner of bird life. Woodcock have been regular visitors to the platforms and rigs since the club started recording such events in the 1980s. It is clear from the club's reports that woodcock use these places on their inward migration to the UK and Ireland but also on the return journey to continental Europe, eastern Europe and Russia. The season of 2003–2004 was such a period, with some notable 'incidentals' as well, when on 11th October and 7th November woodcock were reported from the Buchan A and Maersk Curlew platforms on their way to the British Isles and then, on 28th March in the following spring of 2004, woodcock were observed resting on the Ekofisk platform on their return journey back to the breeding grounds. The recorded sightings by observers of the North Sea Bird Club are fascinating. They range from wrens to a white-fronted goose which was recorded on the FPSO Schiehallion on 5th April 2004. I am no expert on North Sea platforms but I wonder whether some of them could remain after gas and oil production is exhausted simply to provide resting places for migratory birds such as our much-loved woodcock.

However, woodcock do end up in the strangest of places. As mentioned previously, migration studies early in the last century deliberately used lighthouse keepers as it was well known that woodcock are attracted to light. Sometimes these accounts are dismissed or played down through a lack of independent witnesses but, on 6th December 2006, there could hardly have been more witnesses. At St James Park, Newcastle were playing Reading when a woodcock used the pitch as a landing strip. The game was stopped as the bird ran up and down the pitch with the Newcastle centre forward in full pursuit. He eventually caught it and play resumed. That woodcock was released later after Newcastle had won 3–2. This tale was recounted to me by Dave Egan of Corrofin, a keen woodcock hunter and passionate supporter of Newcastle.

Woodcock migration to Ireland holds a particular interest for me. What migratory route these woodcock take is a mystery to me for there is little evidence to show that they are using Wales or England as resting places and jump-off points. Over the decade of this century (but only in some seasons, and it almost defies belief), woodcock numbers appear to increase in Ireland after Christmas and late into January. A good and trustworthy friend, Darrin Gardiner in County Clare, provides such testimony. On Saturday 21st January 2007, he and three other Guns flushed in excess of eighty woodcock for twenty-six shot. In February

2007 he contacted me to say there were more woodcock in his part of Ireland than he had ever seen in his lifetime! He also informed me of a ringed bird shot that was seven years old and ringed in south-east England.

This reference is of particular interest to me. For a long time I have pondered whether, despite the lack of supporting evidence, migratory woodcock use south-west Wales as a resting/jumping point on their way to Ireland. I have always found it hard to accept (as many Irish friends do), that the overwhelming majority of wintering woodcock found in Ireland arrive there via the North Antrim flyway, thus using Scotland and its Islands as their only resting ground en route. This bird, ringed in the south-east of England, surely did not then fly hundreds of miles north, turn left at Stranraer and then flit down to County Clare. Surely it must have flown due west across Wales. Numerous sportsmen in south-west Wales are convinced that many woodcock arrive in Pembrokeshire, rest up and then continue their journey to the east coast and south-west of Ireland. John Bourke, a woodcock enthusiast from the Midlands of Ireland picked up a bird in 2006 that had been ringed near Leningrad two years earlier. This is the second such recovery of a woodcock ringed in that part of Russia to turn up in the south-west of the UK and Ireland. The first was shot by Peter Jones, Llangain, in Carmarthenshire, West Wales in January 1999 and it had been ringed in its first year in October 1995. Was it on its way to Ireland too? We shall never know unless the ringing programmes witnessed elsewhere in Europe are copied here in the UK. We must do our bit!

I find the growing evidence of migration patterns utterly intriguing. Imagine the route this bird may have taken. It was in the Lenigrad district. Did it cross over via Denmark or Norway to Scotland and hence down to the Midlands of Ireland? Alternatively – and I am becoming more convinced of this – did it choose a different route which allowed it to rest up in south-west Wales? Currently, we can only guess, but increased ringing activity of woodcock in England, Wales and Ireland would certainly increase our understanding. There is, in fact, some historical evidence to support this theory of mine. Schenk [1927] suggested that woodcock from the breeding grounds of Scandinavia and European Russia travel south-west until they meet a coastline. Thereafter, they follow the coast until they reach their wintering quarters. Schenk argued there to be three such routes: the western coast route which woodcock from the eastern side of the Gulf of Finland followed on their journey to France, a West Scandinavian route which saw them flying over Danish Jutland and Heligoland 44 miles (57 km) off the German coastline in the south-eastern corner of the North Sea and an Ireland to England and England to France or Belgium route. W. B. Alexander [1939] dismissed these theories out of hand. He suggested it was well known that woodcock reached the British Isles on a broad front across the North Sea. He argued it was not plausible to suggest that Scandinavian-bred birds, on reaching the south-western coasts of Finland, Norway or Sweden, then continue towards the south and head for Denmark, Germany and onwards to north-west France. As for Schenk's identification of the Ireland to England to continental Europe route, Alexander suggests the evidence to be particularly thin! However, I think Schenk was near the mark in his identification of what I have termed the Southern British Isles route.

Unfortunately, Wales was left out from the route described by Schenk and, following his logic, it should not have been. For, I readily accept that woodcock born in European Russia and the Baltic States do, in fact, use this coastal route, especially in the early stages of their migration. From ringing recoveries I am convinced that a significant number of woodcock wintering in Cornwall, south-west Wales and southern and western Ireland are, in fact, using this 'lower British Isles route'. Schenk put this in reverse and suggested a large migration from Ireland to continental Europe. In this, if he thought these to be Irish-born birds, he was entirely wrong, but if he had considered the migration in the other direction – of migrant woodcock towards the eventual wintering grounds – he would have been nearer the mark. There is strong evidence, from recoveries of ringed birds, to suggest that such a migratory route does exist; that birds do, in fact, follow the coast to Belgium, Holland and even northern France before facing the open sea. In 2007 I received details of all recoveries, in the UK and Ireland, of woodcock ringed in the Leningrad district of Russia. Starting with the first that was shot in the south-east of England in 1913 and finishing with the most recent (at the time) in 2007 which was shot in Cleveland, England, there are forty-five ringed birds recovered. Thirty-eight of these were recovered in the southern counties of the British Isles (predominantly in Cornwall, Dorset, Devon and the Isle of Wight) and in Wales (in Carmarthenshire, Gwent and Glamorgan). One was also recovered at Val de la Mare in the Channel Islands. Of the other seven, six were recovered in the southern and western counties of the Irish Republic, namely Counties Cork, Limerick, Mayo and Sligo. One of the birds recovered in south-east England – in Greater London – had flown into a glass window pane, smashed the glass and killed itself in the process.

In amongst these recovery details is the first recovery ever recorded of a woodcock from Russia, from the Gatchina District in the St Petersburg

Region of north-west Russia. This bird was ringed on 16th July 1913 and recovered in Kent, England on 15th November 1913. This particular woodcock was one of an unknown total ringed in the period 1911–1913 by Vladimir R. Dits who was General Manager and Head Chasseur of Imperial Hunting to Czar Nicholas II. This ringing programme was the first one ever to be operated in Russia. It ceased as the direct outcome of the outbreak of World War I when, in August 1914 Czar Nicholas II approved the mobilisation of the Russian military. I would be delighted to discover details of the person who shot it in Kent. As far as I can ascertain, the next recovery of a woodcock from this general region of Russia was in 1979 when a bird from the Prionezhye District, ringed on 7th June 1977, was shot near Derry in Northern Ireland on 15th November 1979.

This, and subsequent recoveries, are attributable to the re-emergence of a ringing programme in the 1970s and from the late 1990s into the new millennium under the auspices of the Russian Ringing Federation. It is difficult to assess the importance of north-west Russia as a region from which we, in the UK and Ireland, receive migrating woodcock since, relatively speaking, so little ringing activity has taken or is taking place, both in Russia and in Ireland and Wales. However, if we consider that, since the turn of the twentieth century, there have only been 290 recoveries of ringed woodcock from across Scandinavia and Russia in the UK and Ireland, then forty-five from the general region of Leningrad is not that insignificant.

However, the problem is simply that ringing activity across Russia has been and is far too low for any conclusions to be drawn. Nevertheless, it should be noted that recent ringing activity undertaken by the Russian Federation far exceeds anything that has been done in the UK or Ireland in the last fifty to seventy years. Moreover, we should not lose sight of the importance of the Dunlossit satellite tracking undertaking by Roy Dennis and Donald McPhee (mentioned earlier this chapter) in the context of roughly supporting Schenk's route B migratory path, which followed the coastlines of Germany, Holland and Belgium. The migration route described on the Highland Foundation website for that Islay tagged woodcock 'Askaig' is not that far removed from the route Schenk outlined in 1927. That Islay bird changed direction twice as she navigated the North Sea, first in a south-easterly direction from Humberside to Germany and second, as she travelled onward from Germany to Olan Island off the Swedish coast in a north-easterly direction. It would be interesting to learn whether she follows the same or a similar route back. I do hope that particular bird survives the breeding season. To my knowledge, her age was not checked when she was captured on Islay and therefore she could quite easily have undertaken this migration route many, many times before and might for many times to come.

Despite my admiration for this work inspired by Roy Dennis, I am compelled to accept that the tracking of one woodcock does not provide conclusive evidence. However, I do find this to be a very exciting coincidence, if that is what it is, in relation to what I have already presented on possible migration routes earlier in this chapter. I am utterly convinced that woodcock from north-west Russia, north-east Russia and Finland follow this coastal route, through Estonia, Latvia and onwards through Germany, Belgium and France, crossing over at convenient spots known to them. From this perspective it allows them a somewhat more manageable journey as it affords many opportunities to feed and rest along the route and reduces long sea crossings to a minimum. Some will, of course, use Denmark as their jump-off point and continue their journey across open seas.

The advent of stable isotope analysis, conducted upon feather samples from woodcock shot in the UK and Ireland, has very real scope to accurately pinpoint their region of birth. Dr Andrew Hoodless of the Game and Wildlife Conservation Trust who is leading this research claims that through isotope analysis scientists will be able to tell which country or region each woodcock is from. For our purposes here it is sufficient to explain that isotopic elements particular to specific countries or regions are extracted from feather samples and matched to an isotope map of Europe, Scandinavia and Russia. There is scope to use this method to indicate the number of British and Irish-bred birds shot in the annual bag of woodcock.

Dr Hoodless also draws attention to the increasing viability of using satellite tags to track woodcock on their inward and outward migration. The shortest routes must surely be known to them along with the more arduous ones from Scandinavia and Denmark across the North Sea. Clearly, they do come to the UK and Ireland on a broad front. However, nature is wise and she would not risk all her woodcock to follow the dominant but perilous North Sea route. Unfortunately, those woodcock that do take the North Sea route are locked into a genetic inheritance that compels them to do so; to follow the same route their predecessors did when the North Sea was nothing more than the Great North River. However, it must surely be possible that not all migrant woodcock that arrive in Kent, Dorset and the south-west of England have flown the length of the North Sea. For example, from Jutland to Margate is a distance of approximately 550 miles (885 km). Given the geography of

Northern Europe it is not beyond the realms of possibility that Scandinavian and Finnish woodcock do use Jutland as a resting point and jumping-off point for north-west Europe.

For example, consider the joint Club Nationale de Béccasiers and French Game and Wildlife Department (CNB/ONCFS) woodcock research and information gathering programme in France. Collectively they produce some fascinating detail on woodcock reproduction rates, age profiles and migration. During the winter 2005–2006 they ringed 4,500 woodcock across the regions of France, showed an age ratio of 65% juveniles to 35% adults via their ageing activities (through the CNB) and concluded it had been another excellent season. Recoveries of ringed birds in 2005–2006 also give some indication of how far they migrate, how loyal they are to particular wintering regions, regional shifts during the winter and the potential longevity of woodcock. For example, several birds ringed in the spring of 2004–2005 were recovered in exactly the same district in 2005–2006, having returned to the breeding grounds and back again. Woodcock that had been ringed in north-west Russia via the French–Russian Woodcock Research Project turned up in Brittany, while birds ringed by CNB/ONCFS were recovered in the Azores, Spain, Ireland and Morocco. One woodcock, ringed in Holland on 7th November 2005, was recovered thirteen days later in the South of France having covered 389 miles (626 km) to do so. From this sample of ring recoveries the three oldest birds had been ringed five, six and seven years earlier, but it was not known how old they had been when first ringed.

There are many sportsmen who do not really expect high densities of woodcock until late November in any given year, but are they correct in assuming so? In the first decade of the present century in particular, we have seen woodcock arrive in significant numbers on the September full moon and each year we have witnessed reasonable numbers throughout most Octobers – but these occurrences are not unusual. These September and October falls of woodcock are well recorded since the start of the last century. In 1903, Richard J. Ussher, writing in L. H. de Visme Shaw's book on woodcock, noted that the north-west coasts of Ireland were the first areas to record migrant woodcock, each year and every year, in September. Inishtrahull, the most northerly island in Ireland, saw them first, followed by Donegal. In most years in my part of the world (south-west Wales) you can almost set your watch by the first arrivals on or around 23rd October but that was not the case in 2007. That year there were some extraordinary falls of woodcock on the September full moon. It is interesting to note at this point that these early migrants to Ireland and Wales are, in fact, distinctly separate entities.

The Irish arrivals are Fennoscandia birds and the Welsh migrants are largely from European Russia, Finland and the Ural Mountains regions of Russia.

Woodcock do not conveniently obey the time restrictions of our shooting season. Weather conditions play a predominant role in migration patterns and that much, at least, we can draw from the experiences of recent years. Woodcock can travel some incredible distances in a twenty-four hour period and if Arctic-like weather does materialise more birds will move westwards. Thus, in such conditions, the birds continue to come after the season has finished. I have never been convinced by the accepted wisdom that all migrant woodcock are on their long-stay wintering grounds by December. Some seasons show the opposite to be true, as significant numbers of woodcock stay in their home regions of Scandinavia and Russia as a direct result of the hospitable weather conditions. The season 2006–2007 was such an event. However, given a late and protracted cold period they will surely not stay there to starve. In the season 2006–2007 there was a distinct scarcity of woodcock in north-west France and relatively good if somewhat late numbers of woodcock in the British Isles. The French woodcock specialists in the French Game Department (ONCFS) were suggesting the choice of wintering grounds had shifted in a northerly direction. Woodcock were found in high densities in Norway and Sweden in December 2006. Was this the result of climatic change? In December 2006 woodcock were still being found in the forests of Russia. In January 2007 masses of woodcock were being encountered at sea level in Sweden.

Historically, it was believed that by December migrant woodcock would have reached their particular wintering region and, after that, only hard, cold weather would induce them to shift. The problem with such a proposition is that those of us who actively monitor woodcock in our geographical areas are aware of regional shifts that take place during the season. However, they do normally remain within the larger, more general, wintering area. Thus, I find it hard to accept the 'here today gone tomorrow' description that has been applied to woodcock. Once they are on their wintering grounds, in Wales or Ireland, they rarely move onwards to other regions unless forced to do so by extremely cold and protracted weather conditions. Woodcock will not simply stay put but will move to find new feeding grounds if cold weather compels them to do so. Even in periods of open weather, clear and dry conditions, the birds can suddenly disappear.

In the past few seasons, in the early weeks of the New Year, woodcock numbers have been stable but we have seen significant increases in the

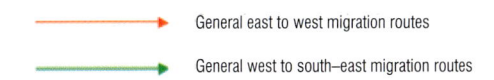

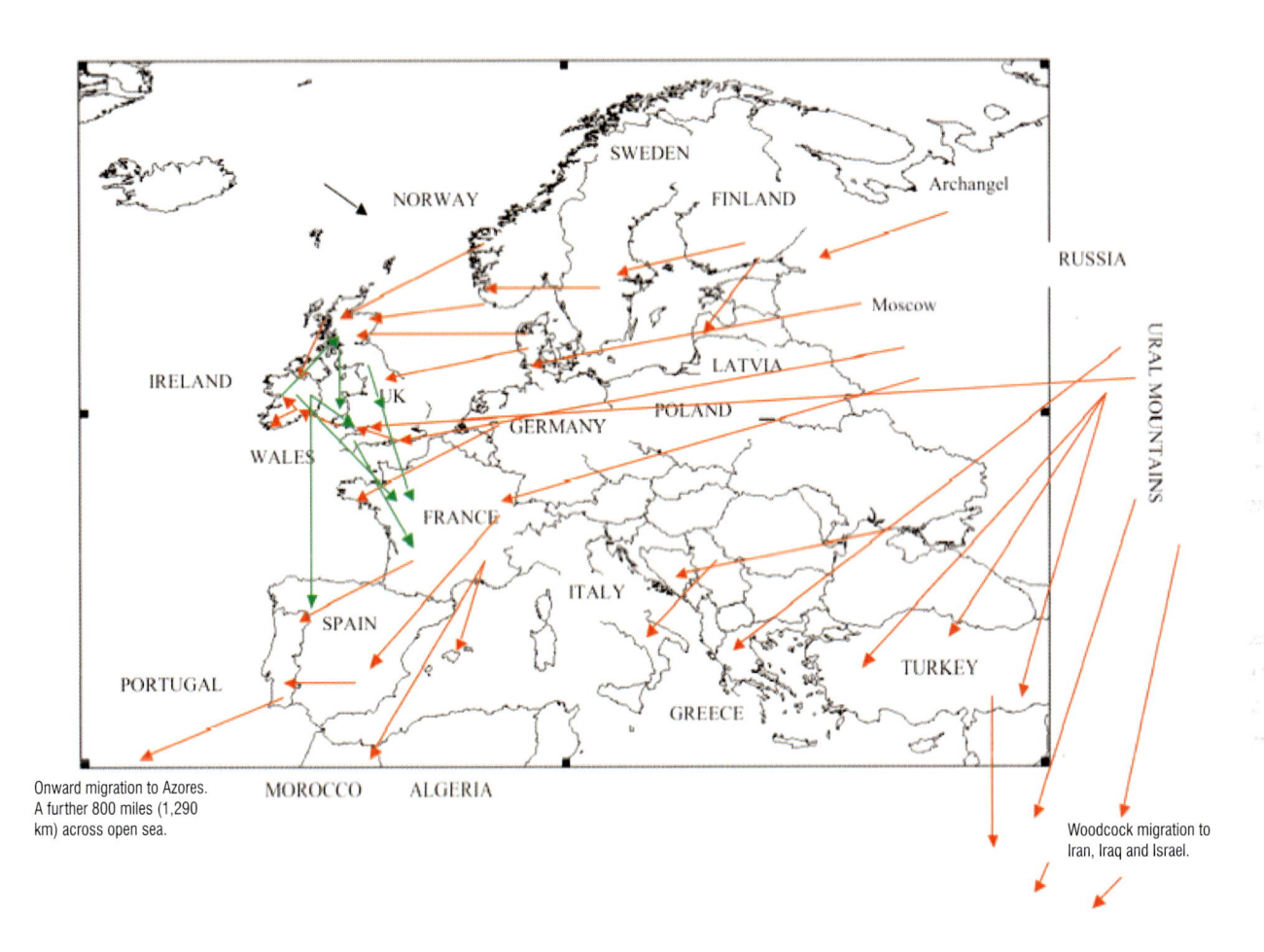

→ General east to west migration routes
→ General west to south–east migration routes

Onward migration to Azores. A further 800 miles (1,290 km) across open sea.

Woodcock migration to Iran, Iraq and Israel.

dying days of the season. In fact, we witnessed some very late migrations in 2007, when huge numbers of woodcock arrived in Ireland in February. On my patch in south-west Wales, numbers fluctuate from week to week as the birds move around the general region and others arrive to infill. In the season 2007–2008, in the week leading up to Christmas, the weather could not have been better for woodcock shooting or for migration. Almost everywhere in the UK experienced frosty, clear days and what wind there was came from an easterly direction. This resulted in some regional shifts and by Boxing Day 2007 my contacts across the UK were reporting encounters with thin and tired woodcock. By the end of the first week of the New Year very few people reported a shortage of woodcock. In fact, some very high densities were being found right across the country. There were huge numbers of woodcock in the south-west of England as a result of 'normal' migration. In the past, a severe cold snap elsewhere in the UK would have ensured a mass migration into Cornwall. In 2007–2008 a staggering number of birds over-wintered in the south-west simply as the result of an excellent breeding season.

In a so-called 'normal' year the first migratory woodcock usually arrive in north-west France around 20th October – remarkably but perhaps not coincidentally some three days before birds arrive in my area of south-west Wales. Are these birds from differing breeding areas in Scandinavia, Finland or Russia, taking different routes to France and Wales, or are they a part of the same migration wave that use Schenk's coastal route first to France and then over to Wales? There is, of course, some evidence of this suggestion by Schenk in the fact that ringed woodcock from Finland have been recovered on the west coast of Ireland. A woodcock ringed as a fledgling on 25th May 2005 at Jurva, West Finland, was shot on 27th January near Ballina, County Mayo. Did this bird migrate in a westerly direction via Sweden and Norway to the British Isles, possibly to Scotland, and then over to County Mayo in the Republic of Ireland via the North Antrim flyway in Northern Ireland? Alternatively, did it use the route suggested by Schenk in that it crossed over to Tallin in Lithuania in a south-westerly direction and then followed the coast until it reached its cross-over point to England, thence on to Wales and Ireland? We could only possibly know, in future, by satellite tagging woodcock on the breeding grounds in Finland. However, shortly before this book was completed, I received a report of a woodcock recovered from Russia. I had netted and ringed this bird on the Gower Peninsula on 31st January 2008. It was recovered on 17th April 2009 near Moscow. I have little doubt that it was shot whilst roding.

Woodcock, under the stress of initial long-distance migration, really do turn up in the weirdest of places. A regular shooting companion of mine, and game chef supreme, Mark Hinge from the Vale of Glamorgan, recounted to me the tale of a woodcock migration in November 2007. This particular bird was found alive and well apparently resting on the steps of a local pub early one morning. Not a rural pub this; not one deep in shadowy depths of Welsh valleys or 'cwms', but in deepest urban Canton on the western edge of the City of Cardiff. Tongue in cheek, Mark suggested to me that on his approaching it, it took off, presumably well cheered, and flew to pastures new. Woodcock are not, in fact, total strangers to the urban environment. I frequently see them crossing the city landscape as I leave work at dusk, or as I wait patiently to be allowed to exit the motorway near where I live. They cross the newly formed urban landscape and lines of queuing commuter traffic with ease as countless generations of woodcock have done before them, following known routes to their feeding grounds. I also see them infrequently as I cross the University campus at dusk and have even seen them feeding on the University lawns after dark, caught in the headlights of my car, which I use deliberately to find them. I am sometimes lucky with those that feed closer to our campus roads than they should. I have also noted from reports of the bird-watching group at Keele University Arboretum that woodcock are frequently seen in the vicinity. In 2003 one was found dead outside the library and it was presumed that it had flown smack into the window.

Year on year there are reports and sightings of 'urban woodcock'. One RSPB 'blogger' reported a woodcock in Lambeth on 11th November 2008 and noted quite casually that there had been ninety confirmed sightings of woodcock in Greater London since the mid-1970s. I would bet there have been considerably more than ninety woodcock passing over or passing through London. These are very old, well-established migration pathways, and bright lights and traffic are not going to deter the woodcock from following their imprinted route map. They do, however, sometimes become confused. A letter in *Country Life* in February 2009 reported a woodcock which flew in through an open window into the kitchens of Simpsons-in-the-Strand. It was caught and released at the Embankment Gardens. Woodcock are frequently sighted in city parks and so-called green islands in the city environment. Recently, one was even photographed in a Hull cemetery and appears on the Hull Valley Wildlife Group's website, looking perfectly calm and collected. I cannot in all seriousness, but with tongue in cheek, think of a better daytime roosting site for a woodcock. Peace and tranquillity assured!

CHAPTER 4

Fieldcraft and Woodcock Shooting

There is a hidden, almost indefinable quality, about woodcock shooting. It may be something to do with the fact that they are truly wild birds, but it is more than this! They are, of course, testing targets depending upon the cover that you and they find yourselves in. It is often the case that there is an explosion of wings, a fleeting glance of this supremo of 'confined flying' and the bird is gone. It is also something to do with the surroundings, what might be called the essence of good woodcock country. It is a passion that is enhanced by the scenic splendor of upland valleys and lowland scrub. In my experience, goodly numbers of woodcock equal peace, quiet, suitable cover and the availability of earthworm – rich dairy farming pastureland or rough grazing in the not too distant vicinity. However, the main influence in relation to where woodcock are or are not is the weather.

Whilst international and national weather patterns obviously play a role in dispersing the migrant winter population, the local weather scene is also an important consideration. Keeping an eye on wind and weather is long associated with this magic sport of ours. An assessment of recent weather patterns is essential to ascertaining where they will be found. Moving from one valley or area to another, east to west or north to south, is often the difference between being in amongst the woodcock or not seeing very many at all. This is the most important consideration in woodcock shooting!

Migrant woodcock, as we all know, appear in October and we stop shooting at the end of January; I often wonder how late into the New Year they continue to come. Weather conditions in between the start and finish of the season are not simply a question of countrywide migration movements as the birds seek out a more clement or hospitable environment. This is, of course, the case but I am aware of similar movements within regions as the birds flit back and forth to compensate for adverse conditions. This is certainly the case in south-west Wales.

Fieldcraft and Woodcock Shooting

Woodcock hunting in upland Brittany. Dr Yves Ferrand and Dr Jean Paul Boidot take in the spectacular view.

Woodcock are not simply passing through on their way to wherever their idea of Mecca actually is. 'Here today and gone tomorrow' is a very old adage in relation to woodcock but is about as useful as a chocolate teapot. Gone to where, and how far have they gone? Those are the questions!

There are probably two general types of woodcock shooter. One is the shooter who infrequently bags a woodcock or two on a driven or rough shooting day a couple of time a season. The other – and this is one I am more interested in – is the enthusiast who almost abandons all else in terms of other quarry in an overriding quest for the greatest thrill of all: exclusive woodcock shooting. It is simply the case that nothing compares to a woodcock in the hand. It is not just the exquisite plumage, not simply a fact that these migratory adversaries are to be admired – the journey they undertake to get here, wherever that is in the UK, Ireland, or other places puts them in a league that few wild birds could match – rather it is the whole exercise taken in its entirety. The search, the dog-work, the anticipation, the double-guessing, the craft and knowledge that this obsessive band of enthusiasts bring to their sport and, above all else, the glorious days of successful shooting in oft-wonderful landscapes, with a couple of brace shared amongst mates, that is what makes it exclusive, the sheer joy of it all!

By now, it should be abundantly clear that I am somewhat keen on this particular quarry species. More than this, in today's climate of political duplicity and political correctness I do not have the slightest inclination to be apologetic for my enthusiasm. In part, my reason for writing this book is to highlight the enthusiasm and commitment that exists for one particular aspect of our shooting heritage. It is not one that I intend to forsake!

The author on the banks of the Odet in Finistere, Brittany.

My love of woodcock shooting is an integral part of my deep-seated affection for and interest in nature. It has been almost ever thus and certainly since my boyhood. I have marvelled at the most basic examples of the flora and fauna of the British Isles. This boyhood enthusiasm has never left me and I have been very fortunate to see it all again through the eyes of my children and to hear the excitement of it all through their voices. The fact that they are pro-active in my world of hunting and fishing, I firmly believe, enhances this appreciation and understanding of the wildwood, the hedgerows, the moors, the rivers and streams and their associated plants and animals. The eye of the naturalist is very often the eye of the hunter too! I fulfil many basic desires in my time spent hunting woodcock. While I take much satisfaction from using my gun effectively, the killing part of the process is simply that, a part of the process. I feel no overwhelming need to quench some inner blood lust. I shoot for pleasure and for the table. However, I get full satisfaction via the other related factors that make up a day's woodcock hunting. To the forefront is the fact that it takes one far from the hustle and bustle of so-called normal life, the endless drudge of 'nine to five'. I have always throughout my working career (which splits nearly into two halves, the first half in industry and the second in academia) worked to live and never lived to work. Thus, work has only ever been a means to an end. Shooting, fishing and the natural world have given me the escape I needed but, more than this, they are vital aspects of my psyche.

Woodcock hunting also suits the solitary Gun and there are times when the appeal of being a lone hunter finds resonance deep inside oneself. Nevertheless, like all gregarious people, I relish company and as I get older I feel the desire to be in company strengthening. For some of the places, even in today's world, are a mite too isolated; the terrain a bit too tricky for someone in late middle age to contemplate. One wrong twist of the ankle, one stumble, one broken limb and one would, in many of the places I frequent, be in serious trouble. Do not believe what the service providers tell you. There are still areas of the British Isles where you will never get a mobile phone signal. I still go to such places, but increasingly against my better judgement. There are some places, secret places, I would not easily or foolishly introduce anyone else to. These I guard selfishly for myself. These are the places I relish. Strange, isolated places, upland areas where no one has lived for a hundred years but where the evidence of former habitation over thousands of years is strewn across the landscape. These are also ancient, mystical places. Long-neglected rough areas, they are the least visited by farmers or other folk. There are to this day areas of marginal land which stand long-

Good woodcock cover.

neglected. Wild places where Neolithic hunters' feet once trod. Woodcock have been coming to these places from the time of Neolithic man and longer. Despite the ravages of the industrial revolution, land loss to industry and to modern agricultural practices, the desecration of a high percentage of our uplands through afforestation, sheep grazing and an unquenchable thirst for mineral extraction, despite our worse efforts, still the woodcock come.

I have shot woodcock whilst standing in the dismantled remains of a Neolithic hill fort, amongst the redundant ravages of Roman gold-mining sites, in the midst of lead- and tin-mining spoil heaps in mid-Wales and off the sides of slag tips left as a legacy to the coal-mining industry. Still the woodcock come, utilising every remaining patch and pocket of cover, searching out and mind-mapping all local roosting and feeding grounds.

As mentioned in the previous chapter, woodcock are not simply birds of the wild lands; they also visit our urban landscapes. Their natural instincts serve them well as they successfully make use of the smallest opportunity to survive and prosper. They are ultimately adaptable. The fact that they frequently use gas and oil drilling platforms studded across the North Sea as resting points is only one example of their resilience. They are incredibly versatile! Woodcock are found in surprising places. I frequently hunt over odd patches of ground that other sportsmen would not blink at. These places always hold a bird or two. I often enjoy a day's shooting by connecting three or four of these 'inconsequential' places into a day's sport, but more frequently use them for the odd afternoon. This utilitarian approach is only a small part of my overall hunting portfolio however. Overwhelmingly, my woodcock hunting is founded on an irreversible, irrevocable ethos. A love of woodcock hunting is a love of lonely, isolated, rugged places; an appreciation of the beauty of tough, hard terrain and of the opportunity to hunt in places that are as near to wild as one can get nowadays.

Thus woodcock hunting brings much more with it than simply shooting woodcock. A love of nature is a useful companion. Irreverence for whatever the weather throws at you is a useful trait also. A day's woodcock hunting is another opportunity to view nature in its wild state. It is also an opportunity to further one's fieldcraft through experience of where and when to expect a woodcock to be in residence, to log seasonal variations, to become aware of how important differing weather patterns are in determining whether woodcock are likely to be found, in what type of cover and at what altitude. Woodcock hunting can and should be all-encompassing. It is for me a passion, not a pastime!

My love of woodcock shooting, my appreciation of the great outdoors, cannot be better explained or illustrated than through this account of two shooting days in the company of a relative newcomer to woodcock hunting in the focused and exclusive manner in which I undertake such activity.

We woodcock enthusiasts, we rough shooters, are very privileged people. We are fortunate that we are able to hunt one of the few remaining truly wild species on the quarry list. The fact that invariably we do this in spectacular surroundings, in some of the wildest, most remote and still relatively untouched places in the country, is an incalculable bonus. It not only adds to the day's pleasure but for many of us it forms an integral part of the whole hunting experience. Each season adds to the bank of memories as we recall special birds, special places and special times with like-minded friends. To repeat my mantra, there is a lot more to woodcock hunting than merely shooting woodcock. Roll on the next season and, in the 'in between' times, we must guard and

The Okehampton Woodcock Club with Captain Barry Fudge (fourth from left in the front).

protect our right to indulge our love of woodcock hunting. There comes a time when you have to 'put up or shut up'. In my case, it related to the quality of the woodcock shooting I have at my disposal.

A casual but nonetheless sincere invitation to the illustrious editor of *Shooting Times* to sample it was eagerly snapped up! Thus, it transpired that early on a very frosty January morning I met Robert Gray (who was then editor of that journal) as planned and bang on time in the motorway service area. There is nothing I appreciate more than a guest who has the good manners to be early, or at least on time. This particular guest, you will appreciate, was a bit special. Readers will understand my apprehension, as they will appreciate the responsibility which accompanies such an invitation. One then has to deliver! It was in this sense that I viewed the occasion, but I admit to being quite excited by the prospect that the then editor of *Shooting Times* was to be my guest for

On the edge of the woodcock wood.

two days of woodcock shooting. Whilst Robert turned out to be the perfect guest and sportsman this did nothing to alleviate my anxiety before we began on day one.

Initially, my worries were those of seeing birds in the numbers I had previously suggested. This concern was compounded greatly by the fact that after a thoroughly depressing wet Christmas we were now in the midst of a biggish freeze. I had, in fact, predicted this to him pre-Christmas but truth be told, I hardly believed it myself! For the week leading up to 'the visit' I was busy calling-in all favours to gather as much information as I could as to woodcock trends given a cold snap. Initially, I had planned to have day one on a local basis but the frost and snow put paid to that as I expected the birds to move to lower-lying land. All that week, overnight temperatures varied wildly from a low of minus 23 °C in north Wales to minus 2 °C in mid-Wales. However, one thing was certain;

the woodcock would be on the move, seeking out more hospitable roosting and feeding quarters. I must admit here that I was ably supported in my deliberations by my then regular shooting pal, Paul. We decided to leave the final decision on actual location until the night before. I can now breathe a huge sigh of relief as it worked out to the letter.

I seem to remember that Robert's first surprise was his realisation that there was a valley in front of us! We had travelled about four miles over farmland as flat as a billiard table and there, in front of us, sloping down several hundred yards on both sides, was the Welsh equivalent of a miniature wooded rift valley. To claim that our descent was steep is an absolute understatement as we held on to the fence and made our way gingerly down the slope. One slip and it would have been a toboggan-like ride in full shooting gear. However, the whole point of this arduous descent was soon apparent as we entered the micro-climate of the scrub-entangled valley floor. Above and outside this secret valley the ground was as hard as concrete, forged so by a week of incessant frost. On the valley floor was another world entirely. There was still a patchy covering of frost but lots of open, damp places where the woodcock could feed. Perhaps more importantly it was warm, much warmer than the land above and offered protection from the bitter east wind of that week.

These places are, I believe, generally classified as semi-natural woodlands in a 'site of special interest' sense. In locations such as this, however, they are simply not large enough to be of real interest and in many instances remain hidden and unknown. The trees in this damp warmer climate, sheltered from the prevailing winds, present themselves as a green gash in the surrounding landscape and are adorned with mosses, lichens, petit tree ferns and fungi. Throughout the farming year they remain relatively untouched. In many places access for livestock is prevented as they are fenced off. These are not places for wandering cows or sheep. You feel this untouched quality to them the deeper you go. No tractors here, no walkers, no agricultural pesticides or herbicidal sprays. They are truly semi-wild ecological reservoirs, too rough, too wet, too steep for sensible farming! However, not too steep for two men and two dogs. Nor for the woodcock either, as they offer warmth, solitude and easy access to feeding grounds nearby.

The choice of this location is a perfect example of what it takes to be successful in hunting woodcock. That is, good fieldcraft combined with local knowledge and an eye on regional and national weather patterns. During that week I forgave myself the inner chuckle as I imagined fellow woodcock hunters twiddling their thumbs up in Scotland as the woodcock beat a hasty migration south and west to escape the worse of the cold weather.

The places that I have for my woodcock shooting are rather special. They are old long-standing woods of Welsh sessile oak intermingled with holly, willow and alder in the wet places, but are relatively open with good, warm and dry ground cover. More importantly, in a woodcock's hierarchy of needs, they are a quick flit away from masses of earthworm-rich pastureland. There is also an omnipresent sense of little disturbance from modern farming methods. The nature and topography of the land, the supreme effort – let alone the financial cost – of clearing these old, wild places has left them largely as they have always been. They remain as crucial indicators of how the natural environment once was. To shoot in these places is to step back in time. For me, it is an environment with which I have had long association, thanks to my lifelong quest of hunting the woodcock.

So I took this eminent shooting magazine editor to one of these places. For him, it was a new but thankfully enjoyable experience. It was very rewarding for me to hear him comment on the variety and extent of wildlife, especially the bird population. He was intrigued when I pointed to the robins that followed us as we pushed through the woods. Ever the opportunists, these robins were on the outlook for any insect titbits that we might have dislodged. They followed us then left us and we were joined by others. I did try to convince my companion that we were being followed by just one robin all day, but I don't think he swallowed that one! However, one of the highlights of the day occurred when a cock bullfinch landed on a branch, just a few feet from where I stood. Absolutely splendid in his winter plumage, this bird struck me as being almost too exotic for the British countryside. The colours of his plumage almost glowed against the background of the frosted trees. A sight to behold and a memory forever! We shared this admiration for what is possibly our most attractive finch. Anyway, I simply love to see them: they cheer me up no end as they add brightness to both the countryside and the day. They come to me, at least, as an often startling but richly rewarding surprise.

However, back to the business in hand. I was eager to flush some birds early on in the day for two reasons. First, it would show the 'guest' that I knew my stuff and encourage him to greater things. Second, it would reassure me that the birds were there in something like decent numbers and give me a feel for the prospects ahead. The first bank produced zilch but I really did not expect much there and if a bird had got up it would have been one of the few that season to do so. Not a well-favoured bank for woodcock but a good starting place to get my bitch, Molly, and the Guns settled. My plan was to work this small bank, interspersed with ground cover of bramble and fern and towered over by some impressive oaks, and then cross over to the sunny side of the valley where I expected the sport to really start. Thankfully, it worked out like that.

I positioned Robert on the bottom edge of a blackthorn and holly thicket, in a spot where, when flushed, dozens of woodcock that season and hundreds over the years have crossed back over to the other side of the valley. I then took Molly in 'through the back door', as it were. The first bird got up immediately and flew forward; no shot for my guest and certainly no shot for me, as I could hardly stand up. The second, a hundred yards or so further on, peeled back to my right! Not a chance. The third was a very fortunate bird indeed. By this time we had moved on a couple of hundred yards into open deciduous woodland. I was eager to position Robert in a good place for a bird peeling down off the top edge of the wood and, as I looked down to make sure he was in an advantageous position, with a 'rip and tear', up it got to my right. I should, of course, have stopped Molly but I only glanced away for seconds. I caught a glimpse of the bird leaving the wood by the top exit. I was relieved that we had started to see them but that last bird should have been in the bag! As we moved on through the wood a nagging suspicion grew in my head; my instincts, born of experience, were telling me the birds were nearer the stream. I kept us to the wood for a further twenty minutes or so but could hold back no longer and took us down to work the cover on our side of the stream.

We had just crossed a boggy patch and, as I pushed my way forward, stooping over to get through, Molly put up a bird to our left. We hardly saw it, but certainly heard it ripping up through the cover. I was becoming a mite peeved with this; four birds and not a shot. However, as we proceeded, Molly put another one up, only yards in front of us, to be lost immediately behind the stunted alder and birch trees. The next time I saw it, through a gap in the wall of branches in front of us, it was the other side of the stream, heading up the bank. An instinctive snap shot at some forty yards resulted in a puff of feathers and that bird was dead in the air. Molly knew so too, ran a straight line, and brought it to hand. Now there are some people you would wish to impress and one of them was standing behind me. His praise was free-flowing because that was a bloody good shot and not a fluke either, as ten minutes later, to muffled mutterings of 'you only get about ten ★★★★★★ seconds to take them', I pulled it off again.

The day continued to follow this pattern as we put up more and more woodcock. However, anxiety number two kicked in. The 'guest' had not fired a shot yet and it was time to jig the pattern in his favour. First of all, I broke my gun, intending to simply work Molly and let Robert shoot, but Molly was having none of it. She sulked immediately and refused to work with Robert as front Gun to me. The only way I could see him getting a reasonable shot was for me to be on the inside of the cover flushing the birds out over him. The first two refused to play the game and broke back high over me. I took both. The third, however, peeled out on Robert's side as planned and he got it first barrel. We did not actually embrace each other but the mutual relief was clearly apparent. Over the next couple of hundred yards we went through our purple patch and flushed a further eight birds never more than thirty yards apart. The shooting certainly hotted up, but with no further birds in the bag. I refuse, on pain of death, to reveal any more detail as to who was in the hot spot. I will tell you only this, it was not a Welshman!

The final phase, the final bank of cover, worked like a dream. The editor, by now, was up with the game and always in the right place. Well, almost always. Earlier in the day, to plaintive cries of 'Colin, I need some help here', I had to go back and extricate him from a bog where he was stuck up to his thighs. Whilst I apologised profusely for not telling him he should work his way around such places and uttered weak excuses about not wishing to bark orders at him all day, I did laugh quietly to myself. Beet fields in the fens are one thing, Welsh bogs another. A quick, sharp lesson nonetheless as some of these places would suck a cow down – and have, of course! But onward, ever onward, as the Bard insisted.

I will never forget the last bird we flushed that day. It was so deep into the ground cover that Molly almost caught it. It tried and tried to thrash its way out and eventually succeeded. In a distance of some fifty yards, given the steep ground, it was at least thirty yards up in the air and going like a rocket straight for the editor, who was hidden from view behind a large hawthorn at the bottom of the slope. A scream from me of 'Coming down' and it went straight over him. To be fair, this was a very fast bird and he could not possibly have seen it until the last moment. His second shot at it and my first shot at it milli-seconds after his simply served to hasten its departure. It is still flying!

Irrespective of the size of the bag – the least important consideration, but of course success is sweet – we had a grand day. The total bag was five woodcock but we both had ample opportunities to have taken this up to at least a dozen. During the final phase, the twelve or so shots we fired between us could not possibly be described as impossible; difficult yes, but achievable also! Some readers may be surprised to learn that we had flushed upwards of thirty-five birds but, believe you me, all of these are extremely difficult targets in confined places and, as other woodcock shooters know, you are extremely fortunate to get a decent shot at half the number you put up. It is the art of snap shooting at its finest if one is to succeed. Sometimes you do not, but this is not a numbers game and cartridge to kill ratios are utterly irrelevant, for one well-shot woodcock in the hand, taken as a fleeting glimpse, offering a blurred patch of brown contrast as a target, is success indeed. The sense of achievement is overwhelming as soft options are a rare commodity in this game.

The location for day two was almost identical to that of day one, only this time we were to work a far larger area. The going was, if anything, even tougher. However, for day two we had the added bonus of being accompanied by my mate Paul and Lil, his cocker bitch. This cocker's ability to find and flush woodcock, her steady, rhythmical hunting style, was a joy to behold. She was a woodcock shooter's dream. Her natural ability would, of course, have amounted to nothing in the absence of the hard work and dedication that Paul had put in. The result was a Wernffrwd cocker *par excellence*.

Our agreed approach was to have Robert close to one or other of us in the very heavy cover and for him to then act as middle Gun in the more open spaces. The day started well as, within yards, we flushed two separate woodcock. I should have had the first of these and Robert or Paul should have had the second. Both were missed. As we worked our way downstream, spread out in a line to cover maximum ground, a particularly frustrating day began to unfold. There were quite a few woodcock on this side of the valley but not as many as we would have hoped. Nevertheless, a number of birds were fired at but with no success. It was a hard slog to reach the crossing-over point, with empty gamebags all round. But again we expected to see more birds on the sunny side. After crossing over we began to flush birds almost immediately. By this time, the three of us were well spaced out on a sloping woodland bank that would keep us busy for the best part of a couple of hours as we trudged along. This is the sort of place where you would possibly wish to have one leg shorter than the other as you attempt to traverse the slope. Hard going, this!

With Robert ploughing through the middle, Paul taking the top edge of the wood and me working the lower slope near to the stream, one would have thought we had all the angles covered. Woodcock, however, are not that obliging! They are, of course, ultra-aware of sound and ground vibration. Given the long, highly sensitive bill they have, I often wonder whether they use it, whilst at rest, as a sensor for ground vibration. I have this mental picture of a woodcock at rest with the tip of its bill touching the ground: a kind of early warning device that lets them know when hunters and dogs are about. Some days they decide to sit tight and camouflage their way out of trouble. Other days, they flit up many yards in front. Whatever the pattern on the day, they have their escape route well mapped out. They use every bush, branch, tree and contour to their advantage – and good for them, I say! This is why this particular branch of rough shooting is so challenging and yet so rewarding. I love it when they jump and swish off at top speed. In fact, I sometimes jump myself, especially when they catch me off guard. This is exactly what the first pair did. As I was busily watching Robert and Paul hunting the slope above, my bitch slipped down to my left and back a bit to a large holly bush. Up they got like the clappers. Perhaps that should be 'up they didn't get' because they came out at floor level. One was simply not a sporting or safe shot with a dog thereabouts and I let it go. The other used the scrub and streamside trees to its full advantage and there was no hope of a decent shot. Curses and more curses!

As we proceeded, a steady number of woodcock were flushed, mainly by Paul at the top end of the wood. This zone of cover received the longest period of sunshine and was obviously known to the woodcock. Both Paul and Robert had several opportunities but these were extremely testing birds, especially for Robert in the middle Gun slot. Cries of 'Coming down' had both Robert and me desperately trying to pick out the woodcock as they came off the top bank and swerved through the upper canopy of the trees. Some broke clear of the trees and were way over our heads as we eagerly sought a convenient gap in the canopy overhead. There were enough chances but most were just impossible, given the speed of the birds and the difficulty of targeting them in the small gaps in the trees above and around us. But, my goodness, this was exciting stuff. If you have never witnessed a fully fit woodcock zipping its way down towards you from a high bank way above, never seen the amazing ability to swerve and dodge at breakneck speed, never heard the 'explosion' as they get up, never fired and missed and still applauded the bird, never felt that warm glow in the aftermath of a successful but difficult shot, never marvelled that you stoned it dead in the air, then my friend, you simply have not lived!

We were successful, however, and managed eight between us. At one stage it was woodcock to the right of us, to the left of us, behind us – the ones the dogs had missed – and even one that decided to join in the fun and actually flew in from our left from the fields outside the wood and presented Robert with a cracking opportunity.

Overall, these were two days when we saw lots of woodcock and, on day two alone, easily in excess of fifty birds. Whilst our collective bag was not huge – not even average, I might add – that mattered not a jot. For it is a rich life indeed that allows one to partake of such fine sport, in such a unique landscape, with good friends and new friends. I know that our editor enjoyed himself; you could see it in his face and hear it in his words. It was a very tired Robert indeed who trudged uphill back to the farmyard. I think the dogs just about had the 'more exhausted' edge on him, but it was a close thing. To be fair this is hard, stamina-sapping hunting. Every damn thing reaches out to frustrate your passage forward, to trip you up or give you a resounding smack in the chops. Every bramble forms a snare for tired legs. Every woodcock waits, a wry smile on its face, to catch you out as you pass behind a tree, a bush, or as you duck and weave your way through the cover. I am convinced that they would laugh at us if they could. The woodland would echo to peals of woodcock laughter because, believe you me, more of them defeat our efforts than we defeat theirs. We see more than we shoot and that is how it should be. However, to see woodcock in such numbers is overwhelmingly satisfying. They are, I believe, bucking most quarry species trends as their numbers are on the up. Long may they do so! The pleasure that I get from all aspects of my woodcock hunting is immeasurable and can only be truly understood by other similar obsessives. I salute them all and, above all else, I salute the woodcock – prima donna of the woodlands!

CHAPTER 5

Tools for the Job

First find your woodcock! This is not as easy as it once was. It is not so much a scarcity of woodcock but rather of available shooting grounds at your disposal. Woodcock are nocturnal feeders and roost in a solitary fashion by day. Thus, good daytime roosting cover is paramount to good localised numbers of woodcock. Whilst the woodcock is often portrayed as a woodland bird it is more often than not found on the woodland edges. There are, of course, occasions when woodcock are found deep in the heart of the wood but in my experience this usually occurs during periods of prolonged wet weather. They do, however, tend to favour more open deciduous woodland. Woodcock need to get into and out of cover as quickly as they possibly can. Therefore, a more open aspect allows them to do this and signifies the importance of clearings and rides cut into woodland. The great woodcock 'shooting engineers' of Victorian days and into the Edwardian era knew this and managed their woodland accordingly. There are few examples of such practice today, but Baronscourt in Northern Ireland would be an exception.

Thankfully, woodcock are not confined to manicured estates as they are far more catholic in their taste for suitable cover. Good woodcock shooting equates to three essential factors. First, a readily available abundance of the woodcock's main diet, that being earthworms, second, good daytime resting cover and third, peace and quiet. In fact, these three prerequisites must meld to give one some decent woodcock shooting.

Woodcock will travel some distance to feed and often change their daytime roosting places. In their study of woodcock wintering in Cornwall, Hirons and Bickford-Smith [1983] found birds travelling up to three-quarters of a mile (1.2 km) to feed. In fact, woodcock seek out and find places of 'superabundance of earthworms' [Hoodless 2007]. For these reasons I am inclined to suggest that lack of disturbance is the most important aspect. In this context woodcock-holding areas should not be overshot and really need to be rested for at least four weeks at a time to allow numbers to build up. I am acutely aware of how fortunate I am to be able to shoot a full woodcock season, two days per week, but still restrict my shooting of particular areas to no more than twice in any season. However much ground you have for woodcock shooting, you should do likewise if possible and rest such areas. Harvest them sensibly, impose sensible bag limits and take pleasure from how many you flush, how many you see and how they jump and fly, not how many you kill. Woodcock are a wild and precious resource! Treat them accordingly.

Woodcock are, of course, found in places other than woodland edges. In my experience over thirty years of woodcock shooting, hedges are also to be highly regarded. There are some days when hunting the usual cover for woodcock fails to produce, but alternatively the birds are to be found on the hedges in some numbers. This is not simply the behaviour of recently arrived migrant birds as I have often encountered such practice mid-season when matters have settled down somewhat. These are not simply any old hedges either. The best hedges for woodcock are the untidy, unkempt, double-thickness ones which offer warm cover at their base and provide good listening and lookout posts for resident birds. Work every hedge at your disposal. Almost invariably, the hedges I shoot have a gutter or small stream on one side or the other. I mention this because woodcock are great runners also. There are days when they flit up fifty or a hundred yards in front of you and there are other days when they decide to run ahead of the dogs. Gutters, whether shallow or deep, allow them to do this, out of sight usually, at surprising speed. I have experienced this on countless occasions. I have actually seen woodcock legging it past me up or down a gutter and they are not slow by any means, which enables them to keep ahead of the dogs and completely fool the less experienced ones. I have seen woodcock emerge from a gutter way, way in front of me and my dogs, run out into the field and then take off. I have also seen my dogs work and work for a hundred yards or more along the sides and bottom of a ditch to eventually flush a woodcock which, experience tells me, was not simply sitting there but had, in fact, run along ahead of the dog until it ran out of ground to do so or decided the best option was to flush.

In these circumstances one has to have complete faith in one's dog and also, even with the best-trained animal, be a bit more energetic in keeping up with the dog because if you do not, that bird will eventually flush out of range. Woodcock traverse some surprisingly wet ditches which one would understandably suppose contained too much water, but

'Waiting patiently'; the author shooting woodcock over Dr Jean Paul Boidot's pointer, Purdey. (Dr Jean Paul Boidot)

when the need arises they seem to overcome such problems of running water. Injured birds are also adept at getting tucked-in deep down in ditches and thus present the questing dog with a bit of task in order to find them. Be patient, trust your dog and go that extra mile to find that bird! You owe it to your quarry, your dog and, if you are like me, to your conscience, as I do not sleep easy when a woodcock has been lost. Persevere, as you are more likely to find it whilst the scent remains warm and fresh.

One of my favourite spots, a narrow valley close to the sea, is dissected by a small trout stream at the bottom. On the one side of the valley there are only fields and hedges whilst on the other side there is rough marginal ground interspersed by large areas of gorse. Over the years it has become apparent that the birds favour the gorse clumps, especially during wet periods. In addition, I have noticed that more woodcock congregate

Woodcock hill with plenty of gorse.

closer together in the gorse, than in the hedges. However, mid-season, when numbers are high, there is invariably a woodcock or two lying up on these hedges. The point is, do not neglect them even when apparently better cover is available.

Gorse, in relation to my hunting of woodcock, has become an increasingly important type of cover. It is surprisingly good at holding woodcock on the breast of hills, on the edge of where pastureland and heather meet. At first sight, gorse clumps look like nothing at all in that they do not appear to afford much cover to a roosting woodcock, but a closer investigation reveals their true qualities. I once crawled on hands and knees, underneath chest-high gorse, into the middle of a large area of gorse, to retrieve a bird I guessed was hung up, and so it was. On the way in, accompanied by a 'face-licking' dog, I was surprised to find how dry the ground was underneath an otherwise straggly, sparse and generally open canopy of gorse – although it could never be described as a waterproof canopy in a holly bush sense. However, on upland woodcock grounds these are the places to try. Often, hill cattle use them to shelter from the worst of the weather and thus create openings and flight ways for woodcock. Hugo Straker of the Game and Wildlife Conservation Trust, a great woodcock enthusiast, once described his affinity for gorse to me by conjuring up the following image:

> My annual sporting travels to the truly wild corners of the Western Isles and elsewhere in Scotland continue to remind me of the key role cattle play in making up a wholly favourable environment for woodcock. Memories of giant gorse bushes on Colonsay which, often umbrella in shape, had been hollowed out by 'camping coos' and with lavish helpings of dung become favoured haunts for the brown marvel.

These are my experiences entirely. These are the places to go on a windy day, especially those high up on the hillsides. My most favourite places to shoot woodcock are steeply shelving hillsides liberally covered with large amounts of gorse – well spaced out sizeable clumps of gorse – interspersed with bracken.

As a result of the increasingly mild winters we are experiencing in the UK, woodcock are increasingly found at higher altitudes throughout the season. Historically, migrant woodcock arriving in October and, to a lesser extent, those arriving in November, have initially settled at high levels of altitude, to be subsequently driven down to the lowland wintering grounds by the onslaught of winter via sleet, snow or frost. In the last decade, such conditions have become less common and an increasing number of woodcock remain at higher levels throughout the winter. For migrant woodcock it thus becomes a choice of using heather, grass or gorse as roosting cover and, in my experience, if it is available, gorse is chosen every time. I am often surprised at how well tucked-in a woodcock can be under low-lying, windswept gorse bushes. Coincidentally, earlier writers on woodcock habits suggested that resident breeding woodcock dispersed up into the hills in August in order to moult.

Despite all of this, my overall advice would be that, when you find yourself in known woodcock territory, you should work every inch of cover available to you. Woodcock are fantastically well equipped in terms of camouflage and consider this: how much cover does it take to hide one woodcock? Without your dog you would walk past 99% of them, even those just sitting atop a covering of dead leaves.

Hunting woodcock out of hedges is a two-person exercise. What you need is a trustworthy, like-minded but, above all else, safe friend. These are usually lifelong affairs! Gorse or fern banks lend themselves more easily to the solitary Gun. Of course, the best cover in the world is next to useless unless one has that essential tool, the rough shooter's dog.

I simply cannot imagine going shooting, whether driven or walked-up, unless I was accompanied by my dogs. My style of hunting, and that of my forefathers, calls for this essential partnership between man and gundog. Dogs are not just an essential part of the team, but an essential part of the day. Watching your dog quest, hunt and hopefully retrieve must be the most enjoyable part of a day's shooting. Surely! But not for everyone, as I notice the trend on many driven shoots is towards an absence of dog-owning Guns. In many ways this leads me to think they are merely there to hit flying targets, which just happen to be pheasant or partridge. The task of hunting up, flushing and dispatching game and the satisfactory weight of the gamebag is left to someone else. What a sad reflection on our sport that is. It is perhaps the fundamental reason why I view myself as a hunter and not simply a shooter of woodcock. Without my dogs I am as of nothing in a hunting sense; I would not be anywhere as near as successful, overwhelmingly so, and I would enjoy the experience of it all, far, far less. In fact I would not bother to go shooting, even if that were shooting over other people's dogs.

A well-trained, close-hunting dog (or bitch preferably – hence the references in this book to several remarkable bitches owned by myself and friends) is a joy to shoot over and adds considerably to one's satisfaction of the day in hand. Alternatively, there is nothing worse than the bellowing uttered by the owner of an ill-trained, ill-disciplined dog that is clearly working for itself and not for its owner. I have seen many of these and have despaired internally, sometimes on an all-day basis, at the constant stream of abusive and four-letter oaths issued in sheer frustration by owners of such maligned, unworthy beasts. There is, in the shooting field, nothing worse than an unruly, disobedient dog. Take my word for it! Realise, acknowledge and accept your limitations as a dog trainer. Invest in your dog's training by using a professional dog trainer or purchase a working gundog that is at least basically trained. You are then in with a chance. You will never regret this investment for, even if it goes pear-shaped subsequently, you will at least have the excuse of being able to blame the trainer, to your friends, rather than having to accept full responsibility yourself. As Guy Wallace once uttered: 'Labradors are born half-trained whereas most springer spaniels die half-trained'. Forego the dubious pleasure of half-training it yourself and get the job done by a professional. After all, you are likely to get at least ten years out of your dog and, believe you me, you will bond closer and derive more pleasure from a responsive, obedient canine companion than you ever will from one that is a law unto itself. You will also have far more opportunities to shoot woodcock and less chance of cardiac arrest.

I train and test my dogs exclusively on woodcock. The premise is a simple one in that, if they can hunt, flush and find a woodcock – a truly wild bird, a bird I believe to be of low scent – then they will easily hunt, flush and find anything else. However, be careful not to neglect the water work as I once did and ended up with a great woodcock dog but that would not, in the majority of cases, cross a stream to retrieve a dead bird. This dog, Molly, once executed a fantastic retrieve on a bird that fell way below me, on the bank-side verge of a stream at the bottom of a very steep woodland bank which was predominantly covered in mature holly trees. It had been a very good shot as the bird jumped through the dense cover of the holly and did not present a target until it was clearing the tops of some very large oak trees. I hit it first barrel, a particularly satisfying shot. It was stone dead and, owing to the nature of the terrain, it fell some distance below me. I managed to get Molly in the general direction of the fallen woodcock and then worked her further away and to the right through hand signals. For once, it all went like clockwork. From my vantage point way above her, I saw that she picked up the scent of the bird as it hit the floor and tumbled forward. I clearly saw her head go down as she picked it up on the very edge of the bank-side and then disaster struck. As she turned towards me, she slipped and plunged right into the flooded stream, whereupon she immediately spat out that woodcock in her panic to get back on dry land. Even though I went down and searched with her downstream for some distance we failed to find it.

However, on another occasion when she was much older and unbeknown to us only two years away from her eventual demise, she carried out an almost unbelievable retrieve from a similar stream. Again, the bird, flushed from the outside cover just on the inside of a wood, went screaming over the tops of some trees, back into the woods, but then rose to clear the trees whereupon I hit it fair and square. This bird was also dead in the air but as it fell I knew that it, too, was about to fall very near to a stream which dissected this wood – or possibly actually end up in the stream. Subsequently, as the dog was taking her time on this bird, I eventually went in to help. There appeared to be no scent of the fallen bird at all and I guessed it had fallen into the stream to be washed away. I was on the point of giving up when Molly went downstream and I followed her down a short distance. Very gingerly, in a slow-motion fashion, she began to make her way out to some flotsam that had collected midstream. I quickened my pace and when I reached the spot

I could just make out one wing sticking up above the surface. Very delicately, she leaned forward and picked it up ever so gently and brought it out to me. Absolutely amazing! That dog really hated water.

Many years later I had another bitch, my current springer, Fern, carry out an almost identical feat. This time the woodcock crashed down through the undergrowth on the side of a very deep ditch, at the bottom of which ran a small stream. She hunted and hunted but nothing came to hand. I went in to see what I could see and she came down the steep side of the gutter with me. Quite quickly, in the one spot, she worked a relatively flat bit of bank-side back and forth, a few feet above the surface of the water in the bottom of the ditch. This section of the side of the ditch was almost bare of any cover and I could not work out what was going on until, that is, I looked to the water itself and there, again, was the top half of a woodcock's wing sweeping back and forth as the water pushed against it. This bird was caught up by some underwater debris and it was a miracle that the wing was sticking above the surface of the water. The dog was at least three feet above it at all times, but had she in fact scented it? My guess is that she had certainly picked up the scent where that bird hit the bare bank before tumbling into the gutter below. Whether she could scent that wing tip I simply cannot say (although Molly, in similar circumstances, had certainly done so) but luck was on our side. Rather than encourage her to go down (since it would have been impossible for her to get back up), I slid down myself and in fact, had the devil of a time getting back up. What makes these feats even more remarkable is that I witnessed both these dogs, on occasion, make hard work of finding a woodcock lying prostrate on open ground. Sometimes, for reasons we are yet to understand, shot woodcock hit the ground with no discernible scent at all.

Such a training regime, such practice, is hard on young dogs as scent is sometimes sparse, and woodcock can sometimes be the devil to find and shift, since they prefer to stick until the dog's nose is upon them, or else run ahead of the dog instead – and they do run some great distances. The young dog's enthusiasm can be affected accordingly. I tend to start mine off by working them with an older, more experienced dog. It is usually the case that, before the end of their first proper hunting season, they will have got the idea, imprinted the scent of a woodcock in whatever part of their brain holds such information and be able to recognise it immediately when next it fills their nose with the odour of woodcock and fills their little souls with delight. If, like me, you are hoping to end up with a woodcock specialist, then this is the way forward. Once they are established on woodcock my dogs miss little else, be it pheasant, rabbit or partridge. Through careful bloodline choice, good care and attention to their diet, accommodation needs and training, these dogs work until they are told to stop. They expect little in terms of game but I would back them against anything with regards to woodcock.

For me, the ultimate woodcock hunter's dog just has to be the springer spaniel, since some of the ground cover and hedgerows to be encountered are not for the faint-hearted pooch! This applies especially to the deeper cover. I am often amazed at how deep into the brambles – another favourite cover-type – woodcock actually go. So much so, that sometimes one can hear them thrashing madly in an attempt to break cover. Nothing bar a springer, a cocker or a sprocker would force their way that deep into cover and with such enthusiasm.

It is well noted in the sporting literature that some dogs flinch at woodcock, refusing to have anything to do with them, but fortunately I have never experienced or owned such a dog. Is this pure luck or a matter of breeding? A bit of both, I think. My current sprocker, Ruby, was one year old when she was sitting alongside me on a gorse-covered bank,

Fern just about to flush a woodcock.

watching my older springer bitch Fern working the cover. A woodcock was flushed, which I shot, and it fell out of sight behind some rather tall gorse bushes further down the slope. It was out of sight to Ruby and more importantly this was the first woodcock she had seen shot. She looked at

Ruby in full flight. A good hard-weather location for woodcock, with soft feeding along the stream.

me and I gave her the command 'Fetch'. She must have watched it flush, fly and fall as she took a direct line down and then behind the bushes. Completely out of sight by this time, I left her to it and moments later, she appeared around the corner with the woodcock and put it in my hand.

I have, in fact, like everyone else, owned indifferent dogs – not for very long in every case – but never a bad dog. My experiences with springers, cockers and sprockers have largely been very positive. In fact, despite my overall belief in springers, some of the best woodcock dogs I have seen were cockers. What they shared in common, I subsequently found out, was a Wernffrwd heritage and they were thus dogs and bitches from the great Cyril Gwynne's kennels in south-west Wales. The old adage of 'you gets what you pays for' rings true here. Breeding is everything and more or less ensures ownership of a useful dog. However, an owner must get to know their dog's line through its parents. Careful selection pays dividends, so do your homework and be clear as to what sort of dog you want. For my part, I want brains and stamina in that order. In terms of gender it is a bitch for me every time as they are far easier to train, being less stubborn than their male counterparts. These are personal preferences and of course there are brilliant dogs out there.

Over the years, I have developed the habit of buying young dogs rather than pups. There are advantages to this as, by the age of six months or one year, their potential is easier to see. Most of mine have been basically trained by then and it is a matter of taking an informed risk, knowing their pedigree and seeing at least the mother. Overall, a degree of cynicism is what is required when one is considering buying a dog at this kind of age.

Nevertheless, it is still a risk and one needs to ask some very pertinent questions of the person who is selling a young dog – the foremost of which is 'Why?' Read the vendor and read the dog and, before you buy, be happy with both. However, it is worth noting that many field triallers do bring a number of young dogs on and, at six months or one year, decide which to continue with and which to sell on. Those that are sold are not bad dogs or useless dogs – they simply do not fit the trialling scene and what is expected. To get some sense of this, always take the dog out in nearby countryside and give it a run and a quick obedience test. I have quite willingly bought dogs that were regarded as not stylish enough or not fast enough for the field trial scene. One of my current springer spaniels is such a dog. She was described to me as not possessing enough drive, as no 'bramble basher', but has turned out to be the finest dog I have ever shot over.

However, I am not entirely convinced that the field trial world is the place that produces the kind of rough shooting dog that most hunters require. These days, field trial springers are predominantly white with a small splash or patch of liver. These overly white-coloured dogs have been bred, so I am told, in order to catch the judge's eye. I do not know whether that is the case but they are very unattractive in my eyes. They are also much smaller, much lighter in build and, as dog trainer Mike Smith described them [Smith 1998: 7], 'softer' dogs than the spaniels I remember from thirty or forty years ago, whether they were field trial dogs or rough shooters' dogs of that time. Colouration and markings are, of course, matters of taste or preference. I prefer a well-marked and evenly marked liver and white spaniel. I am, of course, willing to accept that brains and stamina are more important factors than any aesthetic characteristics, but a well-marked springer in peak condition is a picture to behold.

For my purposes, I need my dogs to be methodical and not simply stylish speed merchants. I need them to be honest hunters; how long they take to flush game is almost irrelevant. I am more concerned with thoroughness than speed, and with stamina over style. Other than the inevitable influences of genetic inheritance which work against a dog's fitness levels and well-being, I firmly believe that stamina can be exercised and fed into a dog.

Dogs are much like children. They are largely what you make them. They do, of course, have individual characteristics and traits and the genetic inheritance mentioned is a determinant with regard to their ability and physical performance. However, little of this inbuilt ability to perform in a hunting sense will emerge unless one develops a good relationship with them. I hope always to be working with a young dog that has the genetic inquisitiveness, the impulse, not only to hunt but to be excited by different scents and smells and to imprint on those scents that count and respond intelligently and obediently. Is this too much to ask? Sometimes, perhaps, but I have either been very lucky or I am doing something right!

Young dogs need to be brought on, to be encouraged; we need to allow them to build their confidence without us losing control. Therein lies the secret, the sting in the dog's tail, as it were. Training what must become a bold, fearless hunter whilst at the same time being able to control the dog in the field on those occasions when it has both nostrils full of the fresh scent of game.

There are some things I never allow my dogs to do. I never encourage my dogs to retrieve stones, nor tolerate them doing so. I despair when I see other owners casually doing this, usually with very young dogs or pups. They should use a dummy fit for purpose, for goodness' sake. I am convinced that such bad practice results in a hard mouth and most definitely results in damage to their teeth. I never let my dogs jump up on me or anyone else. This is an important rule in relation to general obedience but is particularly the case in relation to the dogs sometime, onetime, meeting up with young children. Besides which, I find it a particularly annoying trait as, quite unwanted, one ends up smeared in mud or worse. Last, I have always dealt severely with any dog which is aggressive to others in the field. I will admonish them strongly for growling at other dogs and I will take forceful action if they lunge aggressively at, or attempt to fight with, other people's dogs. I have seen both spaniels and Labradors that, on every occasion, flew at other usually inoffensive dogs as a matter of course. Teeth bared and fangs ready, they had no place to be in the hunting scene. The fault, of course, lies with the breeders and the owners, neither of whom should have kennelled let alone bred from such travesties of what acceptable shooting dogs are. There is, in my shooting world, no room, no excuse for such ill-disciplined, bad-tempered, untrustworthy creatures. The answer, of course, is a higher level of integrity whereby such traits are bred out of working dogs and not just ignored.

It has been over thirty years since I bought a pup at eight weeks old or anywhere near to that age. My only advice is to pick the one you like ensuring that, if possible, it has a good head, straight legs (not bowed like the legs of a Queen Anne chair), is well-marked and shows some boldness. Have a good look at the mother. Other than that, pick the one you like because it is a gamble anyway – and what can anyone really tell at eight weeks? Very little is the answer. From there on it is all about the genetic inheritance, individual characteristics and, overwhelmingly, the quality of the relationship you build with your dog. I am always looking for respect in a canine psychological sense from my dogs, coupled to obedience but not abject fear. They respond but are sometimes required to take the initiative. The rough shooting world is an entirely different place from the orchestrated field trial showcase.

There are, of course, other choices depending upon where you usually shoot – in a terrain, cover-type sense – and also in relation to the hunting heritage of particular countries and their outlines. The great Colin McKelvie, with whom I corresponded frequently on any woodcock-related topic, swore by Irish setters for hunting woodcock. In his estimation they were the equal of a springer spaniel. I did not and do not share that conviction. They simply would not cope with the heavy cover

Setter on point. Nikki the Rocket and the author waiting expectantly in a Finistere forest. (Copyright Dr Jean Paul Boidot)

which dominates most of the places I shoot, which a good springer spaniel would take in its stride. For it is often the case that between the hunting dog and the sitting woodcock lies a dense, thorny, bramble-laden wall of undergrowth. A good springer or cocker will find a way through. They will also do this time after time from dawn until dusk. At least, if looked after properly they will! However, I am sure that in circumstances where the cover matches the capabilities of the breed, setters are excellent dogs for woodcock. I have shot over them in France and I was

Dr Jean Paul Boidot's pointer bitch Purdey on point. The woodcock was less than two feet away.

enthralled by the experience. Nonetheless, the majority of Guns in the UK and Ireland would flinch at the method employed in France.

Throughout continental Europe the practice of using English setters and English pointers is commonplace. Traditionally, the dogs were 'belled' so that the hunter could keep in audio touch with them. More recently GPS collars have been used which, to my mind, appears completely unnecessary. In the winter of 2006, in the company of my good friend Dr Jean Paul Boidot (past President of the French Woodcock

Hunters Club), I saw both setters and pointers in action over woodcock. These were exceptional dogs and I doubt whether they missed a single woodcock between them. The usual practice was that, upon arriving at the shooting venue – usually a large wood – the dogs would be unleashed and off they would go. 'They' in this instance meant two setters and two English pointers. We, the Guns, followed along, listening for the music of the bells attached to each dog. One only reacted to 'silence' as this meant the dogs were on point. When, eventually, we caught up with them it was a sight to behold as the four would be on point surrounding the woodcock, the pointers standing rigid with every muscle taut and the setters always in a 'sitting down' posture, but pointing nevertheless. We, the hunters, stood behind the dogs along the line of point. When everyone was ready, a stone or pine cone was lobbed beyond the line of point and usually, up got the woodcock. These were never more than fifteen yards from us. It was, nevertheless, very difficult shooting as we were usually deep in the woods and the trees were closely packed. It was, for me, very difficult shooting indeed as one had to pick out the bird in a gap (often impossible, given the number of trees) and, being armed with a 12 bore, I had to leave them to go some way otherwise, if I had hit them, they would have been smashed into what I explained to my hosts as a kind of 'woodcock foie gras'. For their part, they were using .410 and 28 bores, often with 24 inch (60 cm) barrels and improved cylinders in both barrels. Therefore, they could and did take these birds at close range. For the French hunter this is a perfectly acceptable and highly effective method of hunting woodcock. In fact, many of them would argue passionately that it is the only way woodcock should be shot – that is, over pointers and/or setters. Many people would question how sporting a method this is! However, the fact that a bag limit operates in some parts of France works to avoid and prevent excessive bags being taken. Overall, the method works because, from what I have seen, the woodlands in France are kept fairly open by the practices of both human and animal visitors. In northern France there is currently an abundance of wild pig and roe deer. Both of these woodland creatures help to keep the ground cover down and during my visits the absence of dense bramble was noticeable.

    The British method of hunting woodcock by using springers and cockers at close distance is alien to our continental brethren. Their physical detachment from the dogs I found to be strange. One never sees their dogs hunting in the dense woodland; one just hears them and then finds them on point. The partnership one experiences close up with a springer or a cocker is not present in that form of hunting. It is effectively

Tom Mptelas's setter retrieving a woodcock in the mountains of northern Greece. *(Tom Mptelas)*

a relationship at a distance – but, be in no doubt, these are highly prized, sought-after dogs. As a method it works in woodland and in mountainous regions. One is not compelled to keep up with the dogs, as obviously they will stop when on point. Therefore, the hunter has a breathing space in which to catch up. For my part I will continue to follow well-trained springers and cockers who work for me, not for themselves, and I will also forgo the dubious pleasure of hunting in the heart of dense woodland. There are, in all reality, enough woodcock elsewhere on hedges, in banks of ferns and gorse to supply me with enough sport – and exceptionally testing sport at that. Moreover, if inhabited by woodcock, these dense areas of woodlands will act as reserves if left untouched. Nevertheless, to each their own!

The other old adage of 'what you put in you get out' certainly applies to the woodcock hunter's dog. It is not just a question of building a relationship with your dog, important as this is. Dogs must be judged as individuals. Just like us they have their traits, idiosyncrasies, wrinkles and crinkles. The wise hunter gets to know the temperament and disposition of the individual dogs. Here, I am more concerned with how we look after our dogs' health and well-being than any philosophical consideration. In terms of housing dogs I would say nothing more than kennel them outside in a spacious run with a well-insulated kennel for winter warmth and ventilation facilities for warmer times of the year. Mine is a purpose-built kennel, not a shed, which has sleeping quarters zoned off by a draught-excluding panel, which also forms one side of an entrance passage at 90 degrees to the sleeping area. It also has a removable roof which aids good housekeeping and can be propped-up during hot spells. My current dogs sleep on a bare floor except in the late autumn, winter and early spring periods, and dogs seem to prefer this as, over the years, various dogs have dragged every conceivable form of floor and so-called dog beds or covering out of their kennel. However, in-between times, when the shooting season is underway, I add differing depths of shredded paper into their sleeping quarters depending upon how cold it is outside. What I use is confidential waste shredded into long strips, not confetti, and this I find to be readily available via friends and families who work for various organisations. It would appear that all is secret these days and whatever the nature of the organisation all waste paperwork must be shredded. This is good news for the dog-owning hunter as this 'waste' is extremely useful as bedding. It has another invaluable use also. I transport my dogs to and from my shooting in a dog box in the back of my 4 x 4. Again, this box was purpose-made to a size that offers them maximum comfort. This box has a mesh panel in the middle which divides the box into two; two independent mesh front doors and solid sides, floor and back. My practice is at the end of a shooting day when the dogs are tired, wet and dirty is to half-fill the box with shredded paper.

Some shooting friends use straw in their dogs' sleeping quarters and transportation boxes. However, having had a dog that had to be taken to the veterinary clinic to have a stalk of straw removed from her eye, and given the fact that straw is not very absorbent and does stink quite quickly with use, I would never use it. Shredded paper is easier to use and is far more environmentally friendly in that, after use, it can be recycled. Mine goes out with all of our other household paper for recycling.

In addition to this form of bedding regime, I frequently rub my dogs down with a towel before getting them to jump into the box. Once they are in the box I cover them over with more shredded paper with only their heads exposed. My current dogs, all three of them, seem to really enjoy this and 'nest' down quite willingly. This not only dries them off on the home journey but keeps them snug and comfortable. Surprisingly they also emerge far cleaner than when they went in.

Vital members of the team.

On arriving home, I always provide fresh bedding in the kennel, again copious amounts of shredded confidential waste, and prepare a hot meal for them. It is vitally important, I feel, to bed them down for the night well-fed, dry and warm. It is not just a moral imperative to look after the most important 'tool' in your quest to shoot woodcock; it also an eminently sensible one.

In the spring of 2008, after fourteen years in the field hunting woodcock, I laid my springer bitch Molly to rest. Imagine the miles she covered in those years of hunting woodcock, often twice weekly, six to eight hours per day. Imagine how many times she faced the cover to flush

Molly with woodcock. *(Simon Rees)*

woodcock. There were never many woodcock that fooled her and even less that she failed to find after I shot them. She did this superbly well for fourteen years and throughout her last season in 2007–2008. The reason for this, as I often tell those who will listen, was that she was better fed and looked after than a lot of children and people are. How fortunate we all are, both men and beasts, in the 'first' world! Look after your dogs, be kind and caring towards them, for without them we are resigned to become static shooters and take our turn at the peg on commercial shoots.

The need for a good dog is perhaps best captured in this message I received from an Irish woodcock shooting friend in January 2008:

> Horrendous wet weather here. Woodcock are about in high numbers but finding them to flush is the problem. Two groups of Guns shooting in the same Burren region recently. One group only managed three birds for six seen to three Guns. The other group of three also got fifteen (twelve by lunchtime). I know these people. It's the difference between having mediocre dogs and owning 'real woodcock dogs'.

Coincidentally, I was also out hunting woodcock in Wales on the same day. The previous night it had been chucking it down but by mid-morning on the Saturday it was more or less dry. Under strict orders to make it a short day, between 10 a.m. and 1.30 p.m. I flushed thirty-one woodcock including three which jumped together. From one relatively small but perfect patch of cover – thick tussock grass overhung by blackthorn, moving to gorse and bracken in places – the size of possibly three or four tennis courts, I flushed sixteen woodcock. In ones, twos and threes they got up within yards of me as my bitch pushed them out of quite thick cover which was, importantly, warm and dry. The reason why there were so many in such a confined space was that nearby there were excellent feeding areas on established pastureland, good warm and dry roosting cover but, perhaps more importantly, this area was undisturbed since the start of the season in October and this was a January day. This one place formed a very small part of a much larger rough shoot of 200 acres (80 hectares).

Fern, my springer, is one of those 'once or twice in a lifetime' dogs who actually works for me, not for herself, all of the time, and knows her woodcock inside out! The best thing I ever did was to have her basically trained, obedience trained, before I introduced her to hunting. I know my limitations. Given an obedient dog I can and do introduce them successfully to woodcock. She is perfectly steady. On this particular day I let many go unchallenged as they were clearly tired birds, but I did shoot five which is enough for me. It was absolutely marvellous to see so many woodcock concentrated in such a small area and to witness dog work of a great standard. What pleasure I get from this dog. She is a rare dog indeed, in that I am the centre of her universe and she behaves accordingly. Biddable, obedient and with a total lack of aggression to other dogs or people, she is the perfect dog. You only have to give her the one command and she responds every time, instantaneously. We never fall out!

To paraphrase the Monty Python team, always look on the light side of life. For more years than I care to remember, in pursuit of woodcock, I trundled all over the countryside armed with a variety of 12 bore shotguns of the side-by-side variety. This was largely more a case of following family traditions than anything more strategic. Side-by-sides were the norm, as was the fact that they were usually over-choked. Over time, I became more and more attracted to over and unders (O & U) and after suffering a permanent eye injury during a day's woodcock hunting I made the move to an O & U. My early days as a teenager and as a young man were times of heavy guns and heavy loads. The main factor which influenced my choice of weapon, any weapon, was cost. Hence, a string of ill-fitting guns that I fitted myself to. I did, in fact, enjoy my early forays with an O & U but at the end of a day's hunting I knew full well the physical cost of carrying 8 lb (3.6 kg) of steel and wood around. Upper arm bruising was an accepted occupational hazard. In fact, I shifted between lightweight side-by-sides and an O & U as the fancy took me. It did nothing for my accuracy, let alone my enjoyment. Then, along came the Beretta Ultralight Deluxe and what a transformation ensued! It weighs slightly under 6 lb (2.7 kg), has chrome-plated barrels, but is choked ¾ and ½. I had mine taken out to ¼ and ½ to become fit for purpose, as such chokes are ideal for woodcock shooting where most birds are taken within less than thirty yards and most definitely within forty yards. Allied to 1 oz (28 g) loads, preferably fibre wad for 'green' purposes, this the ideal weapon for the woodcock hunter who prefers an O & U. It is not just the carrying weight that is important here. The 'swing' weight is perhaps more important. For the rough shooter, sport with woodcock is largely of the snap-shooting variety. Thus, the ability to swing with and past the target is crucial, especially in confined places. The 'pointability' of the O & U is also an advantage here. A light gun, firing light loads, equals effective shooting and a pleasurable day in the field as arms that hang like lead weights become a thing of the past. A well-built gun is a joy to behold, as any owner of a classic English side-by-side will tell you. Berettas are furnished with surprisingly high-quality walnut stocks. I get almost as much pleasure from oiling the stock of my gun as from shooting with it – but not quite!

Tools for the job.

Modern-day shotgun cartridges are uniformly consistent in terms of patterns thrown and quality. However, I do believe that one needs to test a number of various manufacturers and loads to find the optimum cartridge which suits your gun best. My preference is for light loads of 1 oz (28 g). For more years than I can remember I used SMINI cartridges manufactured by Nobel, an Italian firm I believe, in number 7 and 7½. These I found to be ideal for woodcock shooting and much more besides, as they were a fast and hard-hitting cartridge. The only drawback was that they were manufactured with a plastic wad. I have been experimenting with 1 oz (28 g) loads from other manufacturers in readiness for when my stash of SMINIs runs out. I found a very good alternative in the Rottweil number 6½ and I have done equally well with these cartridges in recent years. However, these have also been withdrawn from circulation! Many years ago I was thoroughly happy to use Eley Impax number 6 and would unhesitatingly return to them in perhaps a number 7 if it were not for price. However, as with all my shooting gear and equipment, I will not skimp on price and will return to the Eley Cartridge Company if I am forced to. Their cartridges are manufactured to the highest standards, throw consistent patterns, are made of quality materials and are always reliable. Another alternative would be the Hull Cartridge Company, which produces similarly light and thoroughly dependable loads.

There are some people I know who would not dream of shooting anything lighter than a 1^{1}/$_{16}$ oz (30 g) load. I have, on three occasions, been in the field shooting woodcock as the guest of a Gun who used only 1¼ oz (35 g) of number 5s and, whilst missing woodcock consistently and continually on each occasion, still puzzled what he was doing wrong. Unashamedly, I would still accept an invitation from him as the woodcock shooting at his disposal was first class. However, I would be compelled to decline if I was forced to adopt his tactics for shooting woodcock. Pattern is everything and so is not restricting your success rate with overly heavy loads and tight chokes.

Other aspiring woodcock shooters I have come across were attempting do so with ½ and ¾ chokes. Far too tight! A few years back I spent several days in north-east Scotland near the Loch of Strathbeg shooting wild geese, both pinkfeet and greylag, using a gun choked ¼ and ¼ coupled with appropriate shot size 3 and 1½ oz (42.5 g) loads. I deliberately took those birds I deemed to be 'killable' and did not have a runner all week. In fact, I pulled off some moderately high shots rounded off on the final morning's dawn flight with a left and right at pinkfeet. This I achieved by ignoring, albeit with some trepidation, the advice to go prepared with full and ¾ chokes and maximum heavy loads of BB and number 2s. Ultimately, I put my faith in 'pattern' and the right load for the quarry to be focused upon.

The whole point of this part of the exercise is to shoot well so that birds are killed effectively and cleanly. My style calls for open chokes, light loads and small shot of either 7 or 7½ and these are more than adequate for the job in hand. Anything heavier in terms of choke or shot and load size is simply not necessary for general rough shooting, where most birds are taken well within a thirty-yard range. In much younger, more stupid days of youth, I did on a couple of occasions pull off exceptional shots way beyond this range with the same light loads, but I really should not have fired in the first place as the birds were on the fringe of acceptable killing distance. In fact, most of the birds shot by me employing a 12 bore shotgun could be shot easily and effectively by someone using a .410 or a 20 bore. I had the privilege of seeing such marksmanship in action in the winter of 2006 when Dr Jean Paul Boidot of the French Woodcock Club was my guest for a week's woodcock shooting here in Wales. He shot consistently well, killing his birds cleanly every time, using his 28 bore to great effect. In several instances, after I had put him to stand at the bottom of some very steep slopes, he took some very high woodcock that I would have thought twice about whilst using my Beretta 12 bore. However, I find in the run of things the 12 bore to be more versatile and my Beretta Ultralight weighs less than some 20 bore guns I have handled. Coupled with light loads as outlined, it is the ideal tool for other shooting forays such as summer pigeon on the stubbles, sport which I simply adore, and also for the occasional days when, with some like-minded friends, I take a driven partridge or pheasant day. I enjoy using this gun because it fits me like a glove – because I took the trouble to have it fitted. That is, tailored to suit my physical needs and characteristics. Would you wear an ill-fitting pair of shoes or an uncomfortable suit or jacket? I think not, so get your gun fitted.

My gun fits me so well I am barely conscious of it as I mount and swing to shoot. It fits me so well that I am totally and utterly focused upon the woodcock or whatever the quarry happens to be. Instinctively, unhindered by any dislocation between me and my gun, I take the shot and I am totally unaware of any swing, lead or conscious decision as to when to pull the trigger. At the end of the shooting day I am not bruised or battered because the gun fits and the loads are appropriate. Why beat yourself up unnecessarily with heavy loads and a heavy gun to boot?

In addition, some advice on what should happen next – after the shot has been taken – is in order, I suggest. Colin McKelvie's sound advice was to watch very carefully every woodcock which, after being shot at, continues to fly onwards. He suggested that a woodcock which, upon being shot at, gives 'a curious flick or twitch of its tail... is a sure sign that it has been severely wounded.' [McKelvie 1986: 129]. I have no wish to cast doubt over this advice but it is necessary to point out that in over forty years of woodcock shooting I have failed to notice this 'flick or twitch' from a wounded bird. There are, however, other signs to look out for. For example, a shot at a woodcock which results in the bird flying off with one or both legs dangling is always a sign of a hard-hit bird and must be followed up. One blustery and fine-rain driven morning, with too much moisture running down my face and into my eyes at the time of the shot, I shot at a woodcock and apparently missed cleanly with both barrels. However, as I watched it go – and fortunately this was over flat, marshy terrain which stretched a long way up the valley – one of its legs dropped to dangle beneath it, followed quickly by the other leg. I knew then that it was hard hit. I followed its flight up the valley, still comparatively high off the ground, and watched as its wings folded and it dropped like a stone. It was a long walk to retrieve it, but fundamentally worthwhile. If I had turned my back on that woodcock immediately after presuming I had missed it, it would have been lost to me and would have become food for the resident vermin. We all have a pressing moral responsibility to take good care that we are not wasting this precious resource and be careful not to do so.

Another example was a woodcock that my dog flushed on the far side of a line of trees bordering a gutter we had been working along. I shot at it in a gap in the tree tops as it flew away from me on the other side of the trees. With only time to take one shot before it disappeared behind the continuing line of trees, I thought I had missed it, as I glimpsed it flying on. That bird followed the outside edge of that line of trees for probably in excess of two hundred yards, mainly out of sight, and then crossed the tops of the trees to appear well up but back on my side. By this time it was a hell of a way off! If it had continued with its original line on the far side of the trees I would not have seen what happened next because shortly in front of its original chosen path was a large, thick copse. A further fifty yards in front of me, still following the line of trees but on my side, it suddenly 'towered' and 'towered' at least forty yards up in the air vertically and then collapsed as dead as a stone. I believe this kind of response is thought to be the result of a brain shot. Was that pure luck, or what? Not really I suggest because, again, if I had not been watching carefully it would have been lost to me. I had kept a watch even after it had disappeared out of sight. How many woodcock do we lose by not following shot-at birds until they land again or are out of sight?

The other certain sign of a well-hit bird is, obviously, the puff of feathers one sees coming off the bird as the shot hits. If the bird flies on we can safely assume this to have been a hit towards the rear, in the sense that we were slightly behind the bird when we took the shot. This my uncle always described as an 'arse and legs shot' but really as his favourite 'wind-up' line to us less experienced but sometimes more arrogant young Guns. Clearly, in such circumstances, the bird has been hit and it falls upon us not only to watch it go, but to be as certain as we can that it is not down. If it lands within sight then we should and must follow it up with the dogs. It may get up again to be shot at again or, and surprisingly commonly so, it may be retrieved stone dead or as a strong runner. One word of advice here in relation to 'dead' woodcock: do not proceed to pick up an apparently dead woodcock with an empty gun. Do not put your gun down, as I once did, to encourage a young dog to find and retrieve a 'dead' woodcock. Some of them have a habit of getting up as you approach them. If they fly off some distance, you will have the devil of a job to find them. In the example given, that bird got up very weakly but managed to clear a high boundary hedge. Even though I knew the landowner and had permission to shoot on his land I still had to drive a couple of miles around to his farmyard, as climbing through boundary hedges is never acceptable. We searched and searched all of the hedges on the adjoining property until at last we came back to the boundary hedge. I had been convinced the woodcock had gone much further. With still no sign of it and no hint of scent anywhere, gloom and doom was the order of the day and I retreated into my inner self. My springer bitch Fern must have already nudged my leg twice before I looked down at her; when I did so, there was the woodcock in her mouth. What a dog! How will I ever replace her?

Woodcock hunting involves walking a considerable distance for a day's sport. Usually, this is over very rough and increasingly very wet ground, that not only causes your calf muscles to ache but sucks at your feet and eventually saps your stamina too. Weight carried is therefore a consideration that should be applied to all our gear. As mentioned, there are now several different makes of Italian O & U shotguns that weigh in at under 6 lb (2.7 kg). They are a distinct advantage to the rough shooting woodcock hunter. Alternatively, you could turn to the classic English side-by-side design. However, anything with barrels over 28 inches (71 cm) is a distinct disadvantage as weight then becomes an issue again. In fact, for the sole purpose of shooting woodcock a gun with 25 or 26 inch (63.5 to 66 cm) barrels is best. Coupled with open chokes, this edges close, with its O & U cousin, to being the perfect weapon.

In my experience, good woodcock shooters are largely natural and instinctive shots. Many of the shots taken are at fleeting glimpses, literally windows of opportunity as the birds pass through open spaces in the canopy or flit into the open, momentarily, between the trees. Woodcock are experts at putting all and sundry between you and them. They are not only capable of initially putting a tree between you and them but of maintaining that line until they are out of range. Good woodcock shooting is the result of an immediate yet measured and accurate response: catching the bird in your shot pattern as it goes through that gap, through that hole in the overhead cover, or as it flits over that hedge. It is the art of perfected snap shooting which relies heavily on the speed of swing allied to instinctive firing. Very good woodcock shooters are extremely fast shooters who also make it look easy. However, this level of proficiency is often the result of a great deal of practice.

Of course, first of all, one requires good and frequent access to woodcock in some numbers. I have never been able to answer the questions: 'How do you shoot? Do you give a lead, if so, how much?' because I simply do not know. For my part, I can honestly say I am only aware of shooting at the target but of course I quite clearly understand I am not doing so in reality, as I would then be shooting at where it was, rather than where it is! This style of shooting is closest to that described as the Churchill method. Robert Churchill's method is all about speed and swing. It involves picking up the flight path of the bird, immediately tracking it with the muzzles and instinctively swinging through. In expert hands this becomes one fluid motion, with no conscious awareness of lead, as the proficient individual, mentally, is shooting at the bird. However, the speed of swing invariably takes the muzzles through and past the target. Otherwise, without this achieved lead, one would miss every time. Shorter barrels and a light gun greatly assist the successful delivery of this technique. Those who wish to shoot well and instinctively would do well to consider what Churchill had to say on this subject:

> The great point is that the eyes have nothing to do but to look at the bird. The hands and arms automatically follow the eyes and if the gun is mounted correctly, discharge occurs automatically and in perfect time as the butt comes to the shoulder...Your barrel must always be aligned precisely where your eye is looking. Apparently you are shooting straight at the bird but unconsciously you will be making all necessary allowances...So the shooting man must keep his eye on the bird and ignore his gun.
>
> [Churchill 1925: 37–39]

Oh, easy for Mr Churchill – but remarkably sound advice nevertheless and a very effective method of fast shooting which is often required where woodcock are concerned. One other piece of advice: track the bird with the muzzles of your gun, lifting as you go, swing and ignore the branches. Subconsciously you will recognise your opportunity to pull the trigger. Keep focused on the woodcock. Instinctively, you will recognise the optimum opportunity to take the shot. You will be surprised at the results and assume that you in fact shot it through the branches. This may be partially true but nine times out of ten you have in fact, without fully realising it, taken the bird in a gap. The speed of taking such exceptional shots does not allow us to capture the full picture of what happens. This is very fast and instinctive shooting, the essence of which is accurate tracking and exceptionally fast mounting of the gun, keeping the speed of swing going, to take the opportunity almost before the bird presents itself in a gap in the canopy of branches overhead. Nevertheless, the heel of the butt only hits the shoulder, the so-called mount only takes place, upon the decision to actually shoot!

Ask any woodcock hunter what they would wish to do more than shoot a woodcock and the most likely answer is to shoot two! By this I mean they would dearly wish to achieve a 'right and left' at woodcock. For many woodcock hunters, some of whom are close personal friends, this is the ultimate goal, the ultimate accolade. For others like my good friend, the chef Mark Hinge – who with great motivation and insight conjured-up the recipes for woodcock included in this book – pulling off the coveted 'right and left' would be welcomed, but it is not high on his list of 'must do'! For Mark, flushing and shooting single woodcock provides him with such deep-seated satisfaction and true excitement that thoughts of two at once are almost superfluous. Such a feeling, I suggest, can only be fully appreciated by other hunters of truly wild quarry. Such hunting, that of woodcock included, is the exact opposite of the tameness and predictability of driven game shooting. Also, it does not really suffer from 'sameness' as one rarely knows in which direction a flushed woodcock will fly, let alone what tactics it will adopt next to avoid being shot – and all of this is after you have found it in order to flush it in the first place. However, all of these factors add to the difficulty in pulling off a 'right and left' at woodcock.

As noted by other writers on woodcock, the first requirement, for the rough shooter especially, is to actually find two woodcock in close enough proximity so that, when flushed, they offer an opportunity of a 'right and left'. They must not only be found close together, but also to offer the best opportunity they should 'jump' almost simultaneously. Even then, the direction they take as individual birds ultimately decides whether the opportunity is on or not. In this sense, both woodcock must choose separate flight paths, but flight paths which present the gun with a shot at both birds. Clearly, two birds that are going in opposite directions are the most problematical. Ideally, one would wish the woodcock to jump together, heading in roughly the same direction, not too close together and preferably just a few yards apart. If they were flying into open space or out across the field, that would be ideal and a distinct advantage to the aspiring Gun. Easier written than experienced, I am afraid to note.

It does not end there! I would suspect that the main reason for many unsuccessful attempts lies in the fact that for many Guns presented with such an opportunity, excitement and nervousness affect their judgement and consequently their accuracy. For most of my shooting lifetime, until I achieved my first 'right and left', my knees would turn to jelly as each opportunity presented itself. There were several, or more than several, opportunities. A catalogue of missed chances served to subsequently worsen my state of mind and reduce my confidence. My first opportunity could, in fact, have been scripted by me. Out of the sharp end of a rough and tangled spinney, along which we had been working, Guns on either side, the dogs flushed a pair of woodcock which came out my side in front of me. They got up together, flew out into the open and crossed in front of me from my left to my right. For whatever reason I shot the nearer bird first, at which moment the further bird changed direction quickly and flew at a right angle to its original path, now going away from me. I shot this bird, which appeared well hit and fluttered down amongst the rushes and coarse grass. We picked the first bird out to our right and I moved on to pick number two, feeling more than a little pleased with myself. With the dogs questing back and forth trying to find it, it suddenly got up and flew about forty yards to drop again. On we went and when it got up again I was morally called upon to shoot it a second time, which I did and dispatched it cleanly. No 'right and left' that time.

On another occasion, the dog flushed two woodcock from the middle of a large area of alders. I saw them clearly and the one going away to my left through the trees I shot dead. The other, which I had been conscious of the whole time, was coming straight towards me. By the time I had shot number one, number two was almost directly overhead and, in blind panic, I tried to snap shoot it, only to miss by a mile. Behind where I was standing was a clearing that stretched for at least a hundred yards. What I should have done was to have let that bird go over my head, turn and take it going away down the clearing. Instead, I had the pleasure of watching it fly, unscathed, all the way down that clearing and onwards to safety. Oh, the wisdom of hindsight. I can still see these birds flying.

Up on the Lleyn Peninsula in north Wales, high up on a very steep hillside, I flushed a single woodcock out of the only patch of cover in sight. I missed it with my first barrel but shot it dead with the second. At the exact moment when I broke the gun and it automatically ejected the spent cartridges, two further woodcock jumped simultaneously from the same piece of cover, split apart and flew perfectly over my head whilst I stood there with mouth agape and an empty gun.

There was also the time when I very neatly took a pretty 'right and left' but failed to find one of the birds. This last occurrence is not that infrequent a happening and I probably lose a couple of birds each or

A 'right and left' from the west of Ireland. *(Tony Kiernan)*

every other season through not being able to retrieve them. The majority I suggest are hung-up in the upper layers of dense brambles in most instances and the dogs, whilst being able to locate them, find it impossible to reach up through the thorns to actually retrieve them. I have retrieved countless birds such as these in those places where I could push in to reach hung-up birds. On many occasions, knowing the woodcock to be stone dead but the dogs failing to retrieve it, I have pushed in to see my bitch sitting down beneath a woodcock hung up above her. What a hell of a job it is to push in through chest-high brambles, but I do it every time because I feel the moral obligation to do so; to do everything to retrieve that bird rather than waste its life.

After thirty years of hoping that I would, in fact, take the next chance I had all but given up. However, I had predicted that if I did pull it off it would most likely be the result of two very quick snap shots with no time to think, and so it transpired – and on the penultimate day of the shooting season to boot. Working the lower outside edge of a sloping strip of deciduous woodland, with companions working the top edge, my bitch came out of the cover, ran along the outside edge for just a few yards and literally went rigid, pointing into a very low blackthorn bush with ferns at its bottom. I got the signal immediately and was prepared for the flush when it came. Instead of one bird (as to be expected from such a small patch of cover) two woodcock jumped from under that small bush only feet apart, then split in a 'V', heading back into the wood but climbing as they went. I took the one to my right first as it climbed between the trees. I turned back for the second bird and there it was framed in a gap in the treetops, going away at a slight angle to me and – bang – I got it too. The birds were retrieved immediately by separate dogs. These were fairly difficult shots but luck was with me as that second bird could quite easily have been out of sight by the time I turned, or hidden by the overhead branches. 'As easy as that' you might say, but a long time coming. Prior to this, shouts of 'Woodcock – a pair' turned my blood to ice in my veins. In the period since my successful 'right and left' in 2004 I have, in fact, repeated this feat and gathered the birds on a further two occasions. Overwhelmingly, this later success is down to a more relaxed response as the sought-after feat was already in the bag. In the 2008–2009 season the dogs were in some heavy cover in front of me and flushed two woodcock which flew directly at me, then swerved across my front, left to right, and turned sharply to offer two going-away shots probably no more than five yards apart. I took them both easily. The hardest part was finding number one, which was hung-up in some pretty dense gorse, but we got it.

Over the years I have flushed countless hundreds of pairs and multiples of woodcock. On one memorable (for the wrong reason) occasion I was working a favourite bank of blackthorn on a particularly steep slope of a small river valley where, when flushed, woodcock would inevitably rise steeply on their way to safe cover on the other side of the narrow valley and were usually well up in a matter of twenty yards. My dogs flushed a pair off the blackthorn bank, which predictably climbed high over me. I hit the one and missed the other. I became immediately focused upon cursing and swearing at myself for fluffing such an easy opportunity. So much so, I was not focusing on my dog and she was still in the cover. As I ejected the spent cartridges, she put another four woodcock into the air together. They all roughly followed the path of the first two, up and across to the other side of valley. All were shootable and the two slightly to my right and above me were the easiest pair you could have wished for. I could have cried!

I do not find it that uncommon to flush three or four woodcock together, especially after a recent fall of woodcock (a term that relates to those occasions when numerous birds arrive at roughly the same time in the same locality). However, this is down to the fact that I am privileged to have some of the best woodcock shooting available to anyone in the UK or Ireland at my disposal (often by invitation) and, perhaps more importantly, that I have the time to indulge this pleasure of mine and do so much woodcock hunting.

Overall, the opportunity for a 'right and left' is there for those who are serious hunters of woodcock and even for those opportunist guns who have never sought the 'holy grail' so to speak. One must, however, be ready to exploit such an opportunity and so many factors must roll together to result in success. On recent occasions, largely through tiredness at the end of a hard day's woodcock hunting, I have found myself adopting a more lackadaisical approach than is wise and I find myself pre-judging that bits and pieces of cover will be devoid of woodcock. At the end of one particular day, I had been working a line of trees and thick white grass on the edge of a rough and marshy place, already having had a good and productive day. I barely took any interest in a small island of alders fifty or sixty yards above me. There were only seven or eight trees in this stand, covering an area no bigger than half a tennis court with sparse cover underneath. Having finished working the tree line I turned and, whereas normally I would have moved up to be within range of the alders, I could not be bothered and simply let my bitch, Fern, go up. What a mistake that was. She immediately flushed a pair of woodcock on the edge of this cover and they flew away to the left out of shot. I was more than a bit miffed with myself. I almost turned away but heard another two get up and again I was way out of range. In a final act of showing me what a complete numbskull I was, Fern flushed a single bird from the back of the cover. I still find it hard to believe that patch contained five woodcock and that three of them sat so tight. My own stupidity, I can believe – *easily*.

There are, however, somewhat easier ways of attaining the much sought after 'right and left' at woodcock. A high number of those who claim the prized membership of the Shooting Times Woodcock Club (available to those who have achieved a 'right and left' and have two witnesses to the act) do so through the fact that they have shot such a pair on a driven woodcock shoot or even shot a pair flighting at dusk. I am under no delusions that achieving such a feat whilst rough shooting is far, far more difficult than as a standing gun, whether driven or flighting. When rough shooting, the woodcock which are flushed usually head away from you, but even those that come towards you are most times too close to shoot and must be allowed to travel some distance. Both sorts of flush allow for the bird to put all and sundry between you and it. The really difficult aspect on a rough shooting day is getting a clear shot at one woodcock, let alone two. Nothing is guaranteed and even driven shots have their problems, such as holding one's nerve, as birds are often seen to be coming well before they are in range. Also, standing in a line brings with it additional safety considerations and many opportunities of a 'right and left' have been sacrificed as the sensible Gun will not risk the well-being of his neighbouring Gun. However, in 2008 a remarkable feat was pulled off by three standing Guns on the Buccleuch Sporting Group's Boughton Estate, when five woodcock were flushed simultaneously by the beaters and flew over pegs 5, 6 and 7. To the astonishment of those who witnessed it, the Gun on peg 5 shot a 'right and left', the Gun on peg 6 shot a 'right and left' and, to his eternal credit, the Gun on peg 7 held his nerve and shot number five. Absolutely remarkable and probably the greatest feat on driven woodcock I have come across.

I once stood as peg 6 on a driven pheasant day when a woodcock broke cover at the top end of the line and came over peg 2, peg 3, peg 4 and peg 5, all of who shot at it before I killed it with my first barrel. It was not a difficult shot but some Guns are affected badly by nervousness even when a simple shout of 'Woodcock' goes up and by the time it presents them with a shot they have gone to pieces. Remaining calm and collected is of the essence. Good shooting, I find, is the result of relaxed shooting. Being on a peg along a line of guns can be a stressful experience if one is overly concerned that every other Gun's eyes are on you with a woodcock overhead.

My French woodcock hunting friend and woodcock expert, Dr Jean Paul Boidot of the French Woodcock Club (CNB), simply could not understand the fuss and bluster associated with achieving a 'right and left'. On a day's shooting a few winters back, working a hot spot for woodcock which was a gorse-dotted hillside, I put a pair of woodcock down over him perfectly set up for a 'right and left'. He shot one (he rarely misses) and let the other go. When I asked him why in a slightly frustrated manner, and pointed out the perfect opportunity he had just turned down, he replied in a somewhat sardonically French but truthful manner, that he preferred to shoot them one at a time.

I like to travel light! Of equal importance is the quality and durability of my shooting equipment and, especially so, my clothing. I have never believed in skimping on the purchase of good equipment. I am always willing to pay a fair price for good gear that is actually fit for purpose. On a day's rough shooting I wish to travel light, be comfortable, and remain dry and unimpeded by heavy clothing. Until quite recently I would have thought that the French hunter was better served by his or her outfitters than those of us in Britain. A personal opinion, but over a lifetime's shooting of forty years and more I have tried every conceivable type of jacket and over-trousers. Nothing I have used was comparable to that produced by Le Chameau, the French manufacturer of shooting and hunting apparel. They produce exceptional shooting clothing, especially boots and wellingtons and I have worn their leather-lined Chasseur wellingtons for over twenty years. They are a mite expensive but I have never hesitated to replace them – besides which they do last an awfully long time. They not only mould themselves to fit one's feet like cherished slippers but, being leather-lined, they take a bashing as well. A full zip running from the top down to the ankle adds to their practicality in terms of getting them on and off. In a full day's rough shooting over some tricky, sticky and often broken ground, one's feet must not only be dry and warm but comfortable as well. With my Le Chameau Chasseur wellingtons I never end the day with aching, sore feet. One word of caution however; it is important to take care of that zip by regularly rinsing the wellingtons and applying a silicone-based spray to both wellies and zip. I use Back to Black which is a silicone-based spray for car dashboards but is in fact suitable for all rubber products. You get more spray and it is significantly cheaper than the product supplied specifically for wellingtons, and does the job equally well. Good quality loop-stitched hiker's socks are well worth the investment and add to the comfort factor.

I cannot abide shooting in a jacket of any description or weight and it has to be particularly wet before I don one. Stupidly so, I used to prefer getting slightly 'damp' which frequently meant 'soaking wet' rather than be restricted by the best thought-through jacket. My answer to this particular idiosyncrasy was found via the Irish-based LRActive Hunting and Field Sports Outfitters. They have in their gamekeeper's waistcoat the best bit of shooting kit I have come across in a very long time. Suitably light but made of material tough enough to withstand the rigours of what real rough shooters inflict upon their kit, it is a very well thought out and manufactured product. It has two large external box pockets at the front, two elasticated side pockets, two internal pockets (one on each side) for keys and knife and a gargantuan game pocket at the rear which not only opens out completely but is washable also. It has another feature which I particularly like and that is, at waist level, two sets of elasticated cartridge loops both right and left which hold fourteen cartridges both firmly and securely. Why fourteen I do not know, but that number is ample combined to my cartridge belt worn underneath.

This is my ideal bit of kit, just made for the job. It allows me to travel light, to swing my gun unhindered by restrictive jacket sleeves, ensures I remain cool but not chilled and, importantly, allows me to carry a lightweight waterproof and whatever game I shoot in that enormous but easily accessible game pocket at the back, where both rest comfortably just above my bum out of sight and out of the way. The design and number of pockets also allows me to carry a clicker counter to record numbers of woodcock seen, my Opinel knife (another great French product), a game dispatcher, my keys and mobile phone (switched off but there in case of emergencies) both enclosed in a waterproof zip-top plastic bag. At a push, on rare days a drink and a pack of sandwiches can also be included, but these really would push the weight up and are seldom required. The perfect shooting waistcoat and reasonably priced as a bonus. It negates the need to carry a gamebag entirely.

Caps and gloves are largely up to the individual's taste. However, with regard to gloves, I have always found the open-palm, fingerless, mitten type to be the best. Mine are made of leather, lined with sheepskin and really do keep one's fingers and hands warm on the coldest of days. They also protect the backs of one's hands from the worse ravages of bramble thorns.

Other than this, I always carry a complete set of spare clothing, that is, shirt, trousers, socks and cap, in my holdall back in the car. Twice in recent years I have gone into soft spots up to my waist and, more frighteningly, once up to my lower chest. On both occasions I was on my own. In one of those instances I really should have known better as all the signs were there but being lazy I thought I could get across. There is, as it is well known, no fool like an old fool – or middle-aged in this example.

CHAPTER 6

From the Field to the Table

Earlier, I discussed the sensible harvesting of woodcock and in that context I think it crucially important that we, the hunters, enjoy the spoils of our labours. For too long I simply used the same old recipe for woodcock which, whilst perfectly acceptable, did tend to get more than a bit repetitive. I have reproduced it here but, more importantly, I have also secured the services of my too-infrequent shooting friend and chef, Mark Hinge. The first six recipes, which I have only edited slightly for inclusion here, are otherwise reproduced in the author's original words. They were first published in *Shooting Times*, are truly inspired and the result of a great deal of thought and imagination from someone I know truly appreciates the magic and thrill that is woodcock hunting. Mark just has to be the woodcock's greatest culinary advocate! He has a great love of the woodcock and the countryside in all its mantles. More than this, he is superb company in the field, being the great and completely unselfish sportsman that he truly is. Mark deliberately sets out to reflect his experiences of shooting woodcock, to allow them to influence his cooking in the recipes he produces.

The seventh recipe is, as stated, my own humble offering. Many earlier recipes call for the cooking of woodcock with the guts in place and, in fact, several of my friends eat them cooked in this manner. Whilst I am by no means a squeamish person, I have no desire to eat earthworms, whether fully digested or not. Thus, I clean the guts out of all of my woodcock before cooking. However, *c'est la vie* and to each their own.

Mark Hinge's Recipes for Woodcock

Woodpecker Woodcock

You will not find a green, greater or lesser-spotted woodpecker in this recipe, but you will find good old English Bramley apples, cider and woodcock. The bird is whole roasted and trussed in the continental fashion. Usually, I do not use the bill to pierce back through the 'cock's' legs but, in this instance, one side of the bird's upper thigh had been damaged, so it seemed an opportune time to show how it is done. Woodcock deserve simple cooking and this tasty recipe is easy to follow.

INGREDIENTS

Woodcock (drawn/un-drawn to your taste)
Bramley apples
Cider
Single cream
Seasoning
Olive oil or goose/duck fat

METHOD

Extend the neck of the bird and push the beak through both thighs (see photo). Dry well and place to one side. Peel, core and chop up your apples into segments. Place about a half a tablespoonful (8 ml) of oil/fat in a pan, heat on the hob and brown the 'cock' all over. Arrange the apple pieces around and over the bird and pour in ¼ pint (0.14 litre) of cider. Season well. Cook in an oven at 190 °C for around 25 minutes. During cooking, every 10 minutes or so, remove and baste the 'cock' with the cider and juices. Once cooked, remove the bird to rest. Replace your pan on the hob, add another ¼ pint (0.14 litre) of cider and vigorously heat up the juices, cider and apples. Once bubbling and reducing well add a good splash of cream, mix and serve with the bird.

> TIPS
>
> Dry the bird well or any water inside it will make the fat 'spit'. To truss the bird, pinch the beak shut hard and then push gently through both of the woodcock's thighs. Wrap some tin foil around the legs to stop them charring. If you use an un-drawn woodcock, you could scoop out the dissolving innards and mix up with the apples and cider. Use a medium sweet cider like Woodpecker to balance the sharpness of the apples. If, like me, you prefer a sharper apple sauce, then use a dry Hereford, Somerset or Normandy cider.
>
> Test how the bird is cooking by piercing the breast with a skewer; you are looking for a show of a running 'clear liquid' (well done 30 minutes) or a slightly 'pink liquid' (medium 25 minutes).
>
> Try some seasonal vegetables with this bird. I used mashed celeriac. Boil the finely chopped celeriac, then, when nearly cooked, add some chopped garlic. Drain, mash with some seasoning, butter and a dash of cream and then add chopped parsley, thyme and rosemary. To crisp the outside, bake a 'pat' of it for 10 minutes in the oven. Serve with a hot salad like peppery rocket or watercress. Wash down with the rest of the cider!

Cockbean smoking

Given that lidded BBQs can be used also as smokers, try smoking some game gently for a couple of hours and then serve up with fresh seasonal broad beans and some lemon.

INGREDIENTS

Woodcock (from the freezer)
Broad beans
Garlic
Mushrooms
Lemon
Olive oil
Smoky bacon
Pepper

METHOD

The game (woodcock) has to be smoked under a lidded BBQ or in a purpose-built smoker. To make the smoke, just add wet wood or wood chips. It should take about 2 hours, but check throughout. After smoking, preferably leave in a fridge overnight and slice very thinly to serve cold.

As an accompaniment, quickly boil/blanche your broad beans in water for just 1 minute and then remove to fry immediately in olive oil and chopped streaky bacon. Add your roughly chopped garlic, say two cloves, and sliced mushrooms and stir continually. Add a really good grind of pepper and the juice of half a lemon. Stir in total for about 5 minutes, and serve the beans hot (or as cold bean salad) with your smoked, sliced 'cock' to enjoy in the summer sunshine. I add some grated lemon rind as well, just to give a summer lift to the taste and to draw out the game flavour.

> TIPS
>
> Smoking game in a BBQ is a matter of trial and error. The important thing is to keep the smoke going by adding wet wood chips – even twigs – to the coals. You need smoke, not flame, so keep the lid on firmly. Keep your game off the metal grids! I use a DIY system whereby the skewered woodcock are suspended across the gap between two house bricks placed on the metal grids! Periodically, check during the smoking process.
>
> I do not add salt in the bean salad as the bacon is salty enough.
>
> If you are taking game from the freezer make sure it is thoroughly defrosted before smoking.
>
> Take any washing off the line!

Smokecock

I regard the woodcock as being the tastiest of all game birds and consider there to be something quite mystical and quite special about it. To capture the unique taste and also to be reminiscent of the day it had been shot – which was adjacent to managed woodland – an idea came to my mind. I had caught a whiff of some nearby wood-burning, so subsequently we have smoked woodcock.

INGREDIENTS

Woodcock
Butter
Olive oil
Black pepper
Bay leaf
Rosemary
(Wood chips)

METHOD

Pluck whole. Clean, draw and dry the bird well. Pack the cavity with some butter, fresh rosemary and bay leaf. Tie and truss the bird into a 'sit-up' position with the beak between its legs. Secure with butcher's string or meat bands. Cover well in olive oil and season with black pepper.

Light a lidded BBQ or smoker and, when the charcoals are ready and burning white, add the soaked wood chips. Skewer your bird and keep it off the coals throughout and let it smoke/cook slowly for around an hour. When ready, with the juices running clear from the breast, serve warm.

> TIPS
>
> I used some old pear tree wood chips, which had been soaked in water to make more smoke. You can use any hardwood such as oak or beech but do not use pine as the resin will produce an acrid-tasting smoke. See the 'house brick' and skewers method for smoking woodcock in the previous recipe: it helps keep the meat up, off and away from the direct heat below. You are looking to 'smoke cook' the bird with a warm to medium heat. Check periodically, as the time it takes to will vary accordingly depending upon heat produced.
>
> Some will cook woodcock with the head and neck in place and the beak pierced back into an upper leg. Whereas this is a traditional way of cooking the bird, it does mean that one leg will get cut and will therefore overcook. I truss it, as there is some fat on the neck which will keep the bird's breast moist during smoking/cooking.

W.W.W. Game

There are some ingredients which, when mixed together, make a simple and tasty recipe. This is one of those dishes. It takes the 3 W's, of Woodcock, Walnut and Watercress, for an exciting late springtime recipe.

INGREDIENTS

Woodcock
Walnuts
Watercress
Butter
Olive oil
Salt and pepper
Garlic
Bread
Dried thyme
Dijon mustard
Balsamic vinegar

METHOD

Take a slice of bread and cut into small thumbnail-sized squares and leave to one side. Take your woodcock and, using a sharp knife, remove all the meat from the bone and cut into similar sized chunks to the bread. Chop up a small clove of garlic and leave it also to one side.

Into a frying pan melt a good sizeable knob of butter and add a large splash of olive oil. On a medium heat, gently fry the woodcock, turning all the time; season as it cooks, but do not overcook. Remove the game with a slotted spoon and place in a bowl to cool.

Into the same pan and on the same heat, place the bread cubes (croutons) and stir around to soak up the butter/oil. Add the garlic and thyme and keep stirring the cubes to brown. Once crispy (5–6 minutes), remove from the heat and empty the croutons into the same bowl as the woodcock to cool. Add a handful of crushed walnuts and mix well together.

Into a mug, spoon a teaspoonful (5 ml) of Dijon mustard, a splash of balsamic vinegar and mix together. Meanwhile, slowly drizzle in some olive oil to make a slightly thick 'dressing'. Tip the dressing into the bowl and mix all the ingredients together, to coat all of the contents.

Take your serving plate and cover with watercress. Add your game mixture on top and serve. Enjoy!

Centenary woodcock

In searching for something special for my hundredth published recipe, it had to be the woodcock. Shy, iconic, with a heart-stopping flight, these wild birds are to me the epitome of shooting and conservation going hand-in-hand. This bird was shot in woodland full of wild cep mushrooms. You will love the heady aroma of game and mushrooms/fungi when cooking. Enjoy!

INGREDIENTS

Woodcock
Streaky bacon
Mushrooms
Garlic
Salt and pepper
Truffle butter
Olive oil/truffle oil
Dried thyme

METHOD

Clean your woodcock and, taking a small knife, pierce the upper thigh through in the same place on both legs. Take your garlic and mushroom and finely dice and then loosely fill the gutted cavity of the bird. Take the beak of the 'cock', pinch it together then pierce through both the cuts in the legs to truss the 'cock'.

Place onto two sheets of tin foil, season, and cover in some truffle butter, the remaining mushrooms and garlic, sprinkle on some dried thyme and scatter finely diced bacon over the bird. Loosely seal, and cook at 200 °C for 25 minutes. Open the tin foil, baste and return unsealed to the oven for a further 5–8 minutes to brown. Serve hot.

> TIPS
>
> Truffle butter comes in at around £5 per jar and lasts for ages. Alternatively, you can use truffle oil at £1.50 per bottle. Whichever you use, make sure that there is plenty of fat (bacon) and olive/truffle oil to keep the bird moist whilst cooking.
>
> Pierce the breast to see if the juices run clear for a cooked bird, or slightly pink for a medium roast.
>
> One bird per person is needed, served with legs, head and neck on. Alternatively, remove these parts beforehand if you are cutting it in half to share as a light lunch or starter dish.
>
> Obviously, if using wild mushrooms, make sure you know that they are edible first!

Peacock soup

During January we had a good fall of woodcock into Wales. The little beauty that inspired this recipe was shot over some rough fields, which are now growing peas. Combining the two ingredients of peas and woodcock could not be simpler, but in this case, using dried peas.

INGREDIENTS

Woodcock
Dried peas
Garlic
Olive oil
Salt and pepper
Bay leaf

METHOD

Steep your dried peas in boiling water according to the directions on the packet. Drain, rinse well and leave to one side. Cut as much meat off the woodcock breast as you can and cut it into small chunks. Break off the legs and leave the meat on the bone. Gently fry and brown the 'cock' in a splash of olive oil and some finely diced garlic. Once browned, leave to one side. Take the carcass and boil for 15 minutes in 1½ pints (0.85 litre) of water to make a stock. Remove the carcass and, when cooled, remove any leftover meat from the bone. Meanwhile, empty your peas into the game stock and boil with a bay leaf as per the instructions on the pea packet. The liquid will swell the peas, so stir occasionally and, using a potato masher, crush the peas in the pan as they cook and thicken. Season to taste. After 15 minutes empty the game into the peas and allow to cook through. Serve hot with some crusty bread. Enjoy!

> TIPS
>
> Use one woodcock for two people.
>
> Some dried peas you will have to soak overnight; others just for a few hours; check the packet. Have a kettle of boiled water on standby so that, if the cooking peas soak up too much liquid, you can add more. You can, of cours,e liquidise the cooked peas, but not into a liquid, try to keep some texture in it. Garnish the soup with some fresh pea shoots.

CT's Easy Cook Woodcock

I am a very enthusiastic 'frying pan' cook and if possible use my superb cast iron pan for most things that I cook from field and stream. What I was looking for was a quick and easy means of using woodcock as a starter and simply experimented until I came up with this acceptable recipe. It does not come anywhere near the culinary perfection in those provided by Mark Hinge but it is easy, tasty and quick.

INGREDIENTS

One woodcock per person – breasted and thighs removed
Olive oil
Garlic
Shallots
Diced bacon
Glass of red wine
Crème fraiche
Salt
Pepper

METHOD

Feather woodcock breasts and legs/thighs. Use sharp filleting knife to remove breasts by following the line of the breastbone downwards. Use poultry shears to remove legs and thighs. In a large cast iron frying pan put a large glug of good quality virgin olive oil and on a medium to high heat fry the diced bacon until it is nearly cooked. Add the shallots and fry until they become translucent and soft. Remove to one side. Add more olive oil if necessary. Season the woodcock breasts and legs with plenty of pepper and fry quickly, turning only once until the blood is driven out by the heat. I like mine 'pink' so fry for longer if desirable. At this stage, return the shallots and bacon to the pan, followed by the red wine, season with salt and stir in all of the ingredients including the caramelised bits and juices from frying the woodcock. Reduce the red wine stock by two-thirds and thicken with crème fraiche. Serve hot with copious glasses of a good red wine.

Other than eating them, there are a couple of other 'uses' for woodcock which are worth mentioning. Fly-tying materials are not cheap to buy these days so, instead of just chucking those woodcock feathers in the bin, sort through them and retain those which can usefully replace particular feathers called for. There are several, especially early season spring patterns, trout flies that call for woodcock feathers in their dressing and I generally use woodcock feathers where grouse or partridge are called for, and have always used them to tie my March browns. The trout will never tell the difference.

As for primary feathers, I use them for book markers.

In fact the only woodcock I or other of my friends and acquaintances have not made full culinary or fly dressing use of, are those which I sent to the taxidermist; the first 'right and left' I shot, which look down at me from my study wall, a short-billed woodcock with a beak of just under 1.6 inches (40 mm), another 'right and left' which I shot the season before writing this, and a particularly pretty bird shot by Dr Jean Paul Boidot in Wales in 2006. If it were not for my original freezer breaking down last summer 2008 they would have been joined by the first short-bill I ever shot in Wales, a woodcock that was more chocolate brown than russet and another shot in Pembrokeshire that was grey/black. Alas, by the time they were discovered in an unfrozen state it was utterly too late to save them.

CHAPTER 7

Future Woodcock

In assessing the future prospects for woodcock as a species and woodcock for us as a quarry, considerations of climatic change must be to the forefront. Whilst environmental scientists on both sides of the debate hotly contest whether climate change is a real threat, is really taking place, we lay people can only draw upon our direct experiences and instincts. For my part, I firmly believe that change is afoot and has become more and more visibly so in the past decade or so.

At the time of writing, in the UK and Ireland, the last few winters (especially 2003–2008) have been overwhelmingly wet and extremely mild. In the shooting season of 2006–2007, from October to February, I counted only two days of frost in total in my region. That season, woodcock were cast all over the country and there was a distinct lack of big concentrations anywhere. Woodcock were also being found at higher altitudes than was ever normally the case. That shooting season was a particularly frustrating one as woodcock were moving back and forth between lowland wintering grounds and much higher ground up on the mountainsides and heather tops. To compound matters further, that winter was so mild on the European continent, so mild on the breeding grounds in north-west Russia and Scandinavia, that significant numbers of woodcock appeared to stay put and not migrate at all!

In Russia, ornithologists from the French–Russian Woodcock Research Project were still finding woodcock in the forests in late November and early December 2006. This, in my lifetime's study of woodcock, is unheard of! In Norway, during a field trial in January 2007, at sea level, woodcock numbers were so high they were described to me by one of the participants as problematical. In France, the lowlands of Brittany had a lean time of it throughout the 2006–2007 season, while the Alpine regions of France experienced consistently high numbers of woodcock throughout most of that winter. From my hunting records, I could see that the number of woodcock I flushed in 2006–2007 was 30% down on the previous year, yet I only shot a handful less. There were, however, significant numbers of woodcock in some parts of the British Isles and we did experience further influxes throughout January and into the last days of the season.

From my non-scientific standpoint I can only raise the question that if weather conditions remain open and mild, and food sources remain abundant on the breeding grounds and in the general surrounding region, why should we expect woodcock to come to the British Isles at all? (I am, of course, aware of the genetic impulse to do so.) Conversely, climatic change is also of concern for the breeding grounds. For example, in 2006 weather conditions were not favourable towards high reproduction rates in those areas. In north-west Russia both spring and summer presented poor conditions for breeding. The team from the French–Russian Woodcock Research Project reported a cold spring and a very dry summer. There had been very little snow the previous winter, which resulted in dry forests and high chick mortality (a product of relative drought). During their annual checks on nesting activity and reproduction in June 2006, they failed, for the first time ever, to see any

The author *(left)* with Gary and Eifion Williams at the end of a successful day's rough shooting at Eilean Iarmain on the Isle of Skye.

mosquitoes at all in some forests. On a visit to Brittany in December 2006 I spent every day shooting in shirtsleeves. There were butterflies dancing merrily, blackberry bushes bearing new fruit and even lemons on a tree growing outside in a garden. There were woodcock also, but in far lower numbers than usual. My host, Dr Jean Paul Boidot, President of FANBPO, received daily messages of 'few' or 'no' woodcock from across France.

The 2007–2008 season was also unusual for the high ratios of juveniles to adults in the bag. Some of the bags I examined contained 70% juveniles. Such percentages were common to most parts of the UK, Ireland and France. In late January 2008 Dr Yves Ferrand contacted me to confirm:

> ...the 2007–2008 woodcock hunting season in France has been a rather good one. Indices of abundance are better than those of last year 2006–2007. Migration was normal thanks to cold temperatures in October which pushed the birds to the south-west. So, all migratory woodcock reached their wintering areas' contrary to the 2006–2007 situation. In France the highest abundance was observed in the north-west (Brittany) and the central regions. The hunting and ringing index show a higher preponderance of juveniles to adults but this is yet to be finalised.
>
> Dr Yves Ferrand

In October 2007 I had received positive reports from the French–Russian Woodcock Research Project. Breeding activity was good in June of that year, with unusually high numbers of males seen roding. Significantly, in relation to this discussion on climate change, nesting activity for 2007 commenced at the earliest date ever recorded, in early April of that year. As a result of their netting and ringing activities in the autumn of 2007, the French–Russian Woodcock Research Project was able to show an age ratio of 80% juvenile to 20% adult. This is an extremely positive indication of breeding success. In addition, in October 2007, as is normally expected, the first migratory wave of woodcock from further afield in Russia reached the Leningrad district exactly on time. By the end of October it was reported that migration from central and north-west Russia, as in a normal year, was over.

In 2008, from the New Year, we in Wales once again experienced torrential and almost incessant downpours which left the land absolutely saturated and, in some areas, the woodcock were flooded out of their usual cover. This very wet weather also has an impact upon the woodcock's favourite food source, the humble earthworm. In very wet conditions the earthworms are driven deeper into the soil, thus making them less accessible to woodcock. In part, this explained the growing number of thin birds encountered from December onwards. Some woodcock were clearly finding it difficult to find sufficient earthworms. The other effect of the very wet weather was that the woodcock shifted to well-drained cover and were to be found in high numbers in upland areas dominated by gorse. On windy days especially, such areas produce spectacular sport. However, extremely wet weather does curtail sport and clearly the birds do not flush or fly as well as they would on a dry or frosty day.

In the hunting season 2007–2008 migration to north-west Europe was 'normal'. Seasonal cold conditions in late October pushed the birds from the breeding grounds in a south-westerly direction. Contrary to the situation in the 2006–2007 season, scientists in France estimated that the majority of woodcock had undertaken migration. In the 2006–2007 season significant numbers of woodcock remained on the breeding grounds in north-west Russia and on the coastal belt in Sweden up until December.

Interestingly, in early December 2007, I noted in my game book that on woodcock shooting forays of twenty and thirty years back I would reasonably have expected, by that time of the season, to have encountered many days of hard frost and to hear and feel a crackling underfoot. Those were days of dead bracken, leafless trees and all plant growth stopped. In late November 2007 I came across foxgloves in bloom, honeysuckle in bloom in hedges and roses in bloom in my garden. In early December of that year, I was still seeing bats flying at dusk as I undertook my regular evening vigil watching woodcock flighting out to feed. On 1st December 2007, while out shooting, I came across two apple trees in a long-deserted cottage garden covered in fruit. Three days later, temperatures in mid-Wales, and elsewhere in the British Isles, reached 15 °C at midday. I have fished on colder days in June during my lifetime! The positive side must be that wintertime survival rates for woodcock must be increasing significantly. Woodcock have always been good at dealing with cold spells, even Arctic-like conditions, and therefore these mild winters must see them waxing fat.

In order to protect and prolong our sporting interests in woodcock we must have our own information-base; our own defence strategy in readiness. Unless we are united, unless we possess the counter-evidence, the facts on woodcock, we will be picked-off by the anti-blood sports people, the 'birdy boys' and the faceless bureaucrats. The evidence we can gather on woodcock numbers and trends will be as useful as any scientific evidence. The shooting diaries/game books that some sportsmen keep are of great importance here. I urge those readers who do not keep records to do so – not just numbers shot, but numbers flushed. Gather local knowledge! Are woodcock numbers up or down? Is migration early or late? Besides which, shooting diaries become treasure in later life as they recall clearly good and bad days alike. Having said that, is there such a thing as a bad day when you are out hunting woodcock? Frustrating days yes, but bad days, I think not.

It should be appreciated that, whilst population numbers are not a source of concern, the woodcock is a vulnerable species nevertheless. Woodcock enthusiasts who experienced the fantastic sport on offer in the UK and Ireland in the season 2004–2005, a ten-year high for woodcock numbers, may think I am at best stuck on a fence here. How can woodcock be both plentiful and vulnerable? The fact is, we have to look to the bigger picture, across Europe and Russia, to see what is happening to, and what should not be happening to, *Scolopax rusticola*. We need to do this *now* and not wait until we experience a severe drop in population numbers. Bringing woodcock back from the brink may well be unattainable, not very clever – and it is not what true sportsmen want to see. The kind of shooting pressure that is being exerted on woodcock by some commercial shoots in parts of Europe (including the UK), Russia and the former Baltic States will undoubtedly seriously damage the long-term viability of woodcock as a sporting quarry. From my standpoint, the three main threats to our woodcock are habitat loss/degradation, climate change and over-exploitation.

It is difficult to assess the threat to woodcock if one is not entirely sure what one's national picture looks like in terms of migrant numbers, resident population, shooting pressure and habitat loss. This is where French colleagues put those of us in the UK to shame. Readers may not be familiar with the Club Nationale de Béccassiers (CNB) in France. It is quite simply but quite outstandingly the National Woodcock Hunters' Club of France. It has a structure and a method that encompasses every département (region) in France. In each region a CNB organiser, on an entirely voluntary basis, co-ordinates the club's activities and connects with its members. In this manner the extent and quality of the information gathered on resident and especially migrant woodcock is simply fantastic. During the shooting season woodcock are netted, ringed, aged, sexed and weighed. In an average winter the CNB nets and rings somewhere in the region of 3,000–4,000 woodcock. One wing from each shot bird is sent to each regional co-ordinator for further analysis. This happens right across France via the CNB's members. However, the organisation is active on the European front also and through the activities of Dr Jean Paul Boidot (ex-President of the CNB) we now have the European Federation of National Woodcock Shooting Clubs (FANBO). Woodcock shooters in France are doubly fortunate in that their Woodcock Club is superbly supported by the state funded Office Nationale de la Chasse et de la Faune Sauvage, the Game and Wildlife Department (ONCFS). However, it is only fair to acknowledge that, as a representative political body, it is the CNB that has taken the lead on matters appertaining to the European woodcock.

Woodcock enthusiasts of my generation will have witnessed the loss of winter holding cover over the last thirty years or so. To my mind this has speeded up as agricultural technology has advanced to a point where it is now a practical possibility to convert many areas of previously inaccessible terrain into viable farming land. I have seen this happening in Wales and it is a serious concern for many Irish shooters also. Conversely, whilst at this end of the migration cycle we are still predominantly maintaining our permanent pastureland – thus providing suitable feeding ground – and wintering habitat is, in fact, increasing in some regions of the UK and Ireland, large tracts of suitable nesting habitat are being lost in the breeding areas. As a result of his long-term research on the breeding grounds in north-west Russia, Dr Yves Ferrand (ONCFS) suggests that, as a result of economic forces, agricultural abandonment is on the increase in Russia and the number of abandoned permanent meadows is increasing. Relatively quickly (in five to ten years) these meadows are lost as feeding sites as they become more akin to small forests. This is a problem for woodcock in migration as they previously found their 'fuel' (earthworms) in these pastures.

While there has been a loss of suitable habitat across the traditional or historic wintering grounds in the British Isles as the thirst for more and more productive land has continued unabated, there has been, conversely, a significant increase of good wintering habitat on the upland areas of Scotland, Ireland and Wales. Since before the World War II there has been a steady increase in the total area of commercially grown softwoods, aided and abetted by the more recent revival of a fashion swing towards traditional, natural Christmas trees. In my part of the UK we now have numerous farms which have been completely transformed to become commercial Christmas tree enterprises. What was once poor marginal land is now dedicated to this market and this has resulted in some very large plantations of fir trees which, for periods in their growth, attain an optimum height to act as superb woodcock roosting areas. I have experienced some fantastic sport in such plantations when the trees were no more than 6 ft (5.5 m) high. This is very tricky shooting, but very sporting and rewarding – especially those areas dissected by a stream or two and hunted during a period of cold, hard weather. Woodcock love these places during such periods and are often found tucked in quite tight, as such places protect from the worst of the weather. I have experienced truly superb sport over such ground on that notable woodcock wintering area, the Lleyn Peninsula in north Wales.

In Scotland, there has been a massive shift towards planting more and more softwoods, aided throughout the 1980s by a tax relief incentive to do so, which resulted in huge swathes of the Flow Country being drained and ploughed for softwood cultivation. The situation is similar in Ireland, where many woodcock enthusiasts look to the softwood plantations for their sport as, in some regions, other suitable cover is less abundant. The majority of these plantations have been, historically, those of lodge pole pine, larch and sitka spruce. They only offer sport with woodcock at various stages of their growth. The younger trees offer good cover and good shooting but, over time, the plantation becomes choked by the growth of the trees themselves and by the undergrowth and is fit for neither man nor woodcock.

However, later in their growth cycle, a cutting-back process allows more space and woodcock find them attractive again. Thankfully, I have little need in a normal season to frequent these places. They are the devil to walk in, with hidden pitfalls everywhere, unseen soft spots, ploughed drainage ditches (the edges of which are hidden under the undergrowth) and all manner of other obstacles almost purposely designed to trip you over. Have you ever fallen face-first into a small fir tree? This is not an experience you would wish to repeat as you will inevitably end up in the adjacent drainage ditch as well. These can be seriously wicked places, where breaking a leg or ankle is more than possible. Furthermore, if you think they are difficult to walk and to hunt, try finding a dead bird in such a place. This is extremely difficult, given the nature of the cover, the ground itself and the fact that, often, dead woodcock fall and give off very little scent. Is a 'runner' therefore a better option? Well, for me the jury is still out! You will only find me in such places on days when the sport with woodcock in so-called 'normal' wintering habitat is extremely poor.

I have, however, had some truly wonderful days woodcock shooting high up on the hills in mid-Wales, as an 'outside Gun', with companions working the 'inside' of relatively small blocks of larch. In fact, I clearly remember being quite staggered by the number of woodcock present in one or two of these upland blocks of larch. Their numbers rivalled anything I had ever witnessed on more traditional lowland areas. Interestingly enough, on each occasion that we encountered high numbers of birds in such places, the days leading up to these events were extremely wet.

I have nothing but admiration for those who regularly hunt these places. They are far more resilient, far more determined woodcock hunters than I am. They must also be the owners of some very good woodcock dogs, which are undoubtedly springer spaniels to boot. There is no place in such terrain for the weak or hesitant dog. What is needed here is a strong, intelligent, purposeful hunting springer – or a cocker even – that knows its stuff on woodcock.

One advantage of the softwood industry is the fact that, as plantations mature and are felled, these areas are replanted and the cycle of growth and the cycle of woodcock using them starts all over again. There have also been other forestation initiatives and projects that have benefited woodcock by producing, over time, very suitable habitat. In Scotland, regeneration schemes for native trees such as birch and hazel have massively increased the habitat for resident and visiting woodcock. I have first-hand experience of these regeneration projects and have examined several on the Isle of Skye. Suitably managed for regeneration purposes (of birch especially), and appropriately deer-fenced to protect the young trees, they offer fantastic wintering cover for woodcock and, in turn, great potential for shooting woodcock as they attract and hold birds to the locality. It is, however, a rich irony that in a country devoid of a Game Department, British sport is nevertheless enhanced – albeit by a process of default – by governmental initiatives and funding not purposely designed to do so. The Scottish Forest Alliance – which includes petroleum giant BP, the Forestry Commission Scotland, the Woodland Trust and the RSPB Scotland – aims to regenerate and expand native woodlands by approximately 30,000 acres (12,150 hectares) by encouraging the planting of 2.7 million trees. This will be the result of a total financial commitment of £30 million by the year of this book's publication (2010). It can only be good news for our native fauna and flora, including the woodcock. In addition, there are hundreds of thousands of hectares of public/private initiatives across Scotland's farming and shooting estates where similar regeneration projects are in place. In Wales, the 'Tir Gofal' agri-environment scheme via the Welsh Assembly Government has, at the time of writing, secured the participation of 3,000 farmers and covers 741,300 acres (300,000 hectares) of land. A core part of this scheme is the fencing-off and protection of native woodland areas of all sizes from small copses to large woods. Undisturbed by livestock, they act as perfect resting and roosting areas for woodcock.

The point should not be lost that all these examples of increasing and protecting native woodlands do not just add to the wintering habitat but also, potentially, increase the nesting and breeding areas available to woodcock. Unlike their softwood counterparts, these areas of regenerated native woodland offer ideal habitat for both purposes. As such, they are probably the most significant habitat development, in a woodcock conservation and sustainability sense, for nearly a century. It has been almost a hundred years since we witnessed the deliberate planting of stands of timber by woodcock-shooting wealthy landowners in the west of Ireland. There, woodland management was optimised to attract and retain woodcock. It is to be hoped that current-day agri-environmental and regeneration programmes will have the same impact. I am confident they will. In fact, I suspect that resident breeding numbers in the UK in particular are already at an all-time high. This view is shared by many other woodcock hunters across the UK and Ireland. In the last five years prior to writing this I have had more reports of nesting woodcock than ever before. As mentioned previously, however, what is required is a well-structured, suitably funded project that collects and collates this information. In his letter to *The Field* in 2004, Colin McKelvie pointed out the significance of these developments. He suggested that, by then, the regeneration of native species in Scotland had grown to encompass tens of thousands of hectares of what had been nothing more than rough hill grazing and bog land in the 1980s. In his estimation this had resulted in excellent woodcock wintering habitat as a direct outcome of this regeneration programme. He went to emphasise the fact that:

> ...newly created woodcock wintering habitat now exists in many places for the first time in centuries, and those who shoot there are consistently finding excellent numbers of woodcock.
>
> [McKelvie 2004]

Shooting pressure on woodcock, in the UK and Ireland, is far less than it is in France and elsewhere in the European Union. The scientists at the

ONCFS in France have been monitoring woodcock and forming data sets for the last twenty years or more. In 2008, drawing upon this longitudinal analysis, Ferrand et al. of the ONCFS estimated an annual bag of woodcock from across France as being in the region of 1.2 million birds and, across Europe, a figure of 3–4 million. The data set employed to assess population dynamics draws upon several means of assessment. The ONCFS scientists, and volunteers from the CNB, undertake annual monitoring programmes of the breeding population across France (through observations of roding males) and on the wintering population (through a census of numbers of woodcock flushed and shot on hunting days). In addition, their ringing programme is a prime source of information too. Currently, 3,000–4,000 woodcock are ringed annually across France and, since 1998, this has enabled the French researchers to amass a database which currently includes 40,000 ringed birds, 7,000 recoveries of ringed birds and 2,500 recaptures [Ferrand et al. (article on monitoring French populations) 2008]. Apparently, there are approximately 1,500 volunteers involved in this initiative and these numbers also include some 300 specialised ringers. At the time of writing, I am only aware of eight woodcock ringers in the whole of the UK and Ireland, and four of these are still trainees.

Ferrand and his colleagues suggest that the hunting bag estimate is somewhat out of date as the last assessment took place in 1999. However, at that time, it was suggested that 300,000 French hunters shot at least one woodcock each season and that somewhere in the region of 28,000 hunters shot more than ten birds. The bag of those deemed to be 'specialists', who shot more than ten birds each, was estimated to be near to 500,000 woodcock. More importantly, Ferrand et al. draw attention to the growth in 'specialists', which had increased by 2.9% by 1999. This led them to conclude that hunting pressure in France was (and probably still is) increasing. However, there are two issues here that are worthy of further exploration in my assessment of a sustainable future for woodcock. First, I think the estimated annual bag of woodcock in France is underplayed, overly conservative and has inherent problems. What exactly does ten or more birds shot actually give us in terms of hard evidence? Some hunters, shooting twice a week throughout the hunting season, would surely shoot far more than ten woodcock. Bag limits only appertain to the Brittany region of France. Some of those individuals could have shot a hundred or more. Second, the hunting community is notorious for its unwillingness to provide hard data on its hunting activities and outcomes.

Nevertheless, this French assessment is a very important one for

European hunters as it is the only integrated scheme of study currently available to us. It not only assesses breeding and wintering populations in France, but also draws upon its collaborative research with Russian scientists at St Petersburg State University and the State Informational Analytical Centre for Game and the Environment of Moscow. This Russian-based programme is based upon a 'listening sites' project, whereby roding males are identify and logged and also, in the autumn of each year, by a netting and ringing programme of woodcock at the start of their migratory journey westwards. This also allows them to give an indication of breeding success in that year by ageing the woodcock into juveniles and adults. Furthermore, it allows an assessment of survival rates as some of the previously ringed birds are recaptured. However, given the geographical extent of the breeding grounds and the massive migratory front available to the woodcock, this is at best a very useful and informative exercise, but nonetheless a mere snapshot of what is happening on a small area of the overall breeding grounds in north-west Russia.

Of greater concern, is the French team's evidence that whilst deciduous woodland is increasing across Europe (thus providing more potential roosting and nesting cover, as discussed earlier in specific relation to the British Isles), meadow areas, vital for producing abundant sources of earthworms and thus sufficient food for woodcock, have been declining quite drastically in some regions of the European Union – driven, no doubt, by the Common Agricultural Policy. The authors suggest that over a quarter (25%) of available meadowland was lost in France – to cereal production largely – in the period 1970–1995 [Ferrand et al. (article on monitoring French populations) 2008: 50]. However, their conclusion, based upon a mass of scientific evidence collected over a period of twenty years of research up to 2008, is that the breeding population in France is stable and not decreasing, the wintering population from Russia is stable and that, whilst hunting bags appear stable, hunting pressure may have increased. This last point is of greatest concern in a French context as the true picture in relation to overall hunting pressure is difficult to see and remains largely hidden. For another eminent woodcock scientist and hunter, Dr Jean Paul Boidot, past President of the CNB and current President of the European Federation of woodcock Hunting Clubs (FANBPO) the most serious current threats to Woodcock are over-exploitation by commercial shooting interests (thus the agreed bag limit on woodcock in all districts in Brittany), the loss of permanent meadows to cereal production, and climate change, which drastically affects breeding success rates both in European countries and in north-west Russia.

In the UK, this kind of assessment of woodcock facts and figures has historically been carried out by the Game and Wildlife Conservation Trust, in its former guise as the Game Conservancy Trust, through its National Gamebag Census. In its most current assessment (2008), the GWCT concluded that barely any negative change in woodcock numbers could be detected over the duration of the twentieth century. Drawing upon data on woodcock gathered from 1,290 shoots, predominantly in England, for the period 1900–2002, the GWCT suggests that woodcock bag numbers were, in fact, higher for the last quarter of the twentieth century than they were for the first quarter. More importantly, they argue that the conservation status of woodcock has been misjudged. In my estimation (as I have argued elsewhere in this book), the conservation status of woodcock has been seriously misjudged and it is interesting to note that, whilst I have been arguing this since 2000, it is only recently (2008) that the GWCT has revised both its figures on woodcock in general and resident breeders in particular!

These shoot reports are, of course, useful but only present a partial account. They are not the only or best source of information on woodcock in the gamebag or in a general trend context, as they do not capture the information held by the rough shooter or the woodcock 'specialist' of the French example. There has not been (there is still not) any concerted attempt, any structured attempt, to draw upon the recorded or remembered evidence of generations of woodcock shooters in the British Isles. There have been some brief forays by organisations like the then-named Wildfowlers Association of Great Britain and Ireland to gather information on woodcock through its wings survey, but nothing that really compares to the joined-up research and assessment programmes that exist in France, which encourage and enable effective collaboration between the scientific community and the hunter.

However, there is a wealth of information out there waiting to be collated. For example, the Camddwr Shooting Society, historically a farmer's shoot in mid-Wales, was established back in the early 1960s and its shoot records contain some interesting facts on woodcock. It is predominantly a 'walk and stand' shoot whereby the Guns alternate between shooting and beating. On average, the society releases 500–600 pheasants each year but of greater significance is the fact that it is also a great place for high numbers of wintering woodcock. It is, in fact, one of those rare venues where reared pheasant activity appears to have little impact upon wintering woodcock numbers. It is generally the case that intensive game bird rearing practices do have a detrimental effect on wintering woodcock numbers over that ground. However, on the

Camddwr shoot this is not the case and over recent years the numbers of woodcock flushed have been reported as quite spectacular. From what I know of this shoot, this is the outcome of a number of factors which combine to produce very high numbers of wintering woodcock. First, the shooting pressure via reared pheasants is low and complemented by the 'stand and shoot' practice adopted. There are only eighteen members in the society. Second, the shoot extends to over 300 acres (122 hectares) and the terrain is conducive to affording woodcock much peace and tranquillity outside of shoot days. Third, and probably more importantly, is the fact that the habitat is favourable to woodcock.

Whilst the society has shoot records going back to the 1961–1962 season, it is interesting to note the returns for woodcock for the twelve years up to 209 – see Table 1. What is notable and obvious is the gradual but significant increase in the annual woodcock bag since 1997–1998 (28 birds) to a current high in the 2008–2009 shooting season when 135 were shot. For club secretary Michael Williams, the increased number of woodcock flushed and shot is the direct result of the habitat improvement work that has taken place over the last decade or so.

TABLE 1

Camddwr Shooting Society Woodcock Records 1997–2009

1997–1998	28	2003–2004	35
1998–1999	35	2004–2005	98
1999–2000	36	2005–2006	107
2000–2001	45	2006–2007	81
2001–2002	70	2007–2008	120
2002–2003	50	2008–2009	135

[Camddwr Shooting Society 2009]

A particularly rich source of information and recorded data on woodcock is, I suspect, being held by members of the National Association of Regional Game Councils of Ireland (NARGC). With a membership at the time of writing of 27,000, mainly rough shooting members, in 840 Gun Clubs spread across Ireland, organised into twenty-eight regions, it has the potential to deliver a mass of information each year on woodcock across Ireland both in and out of the shooting season. It not only stores a wealth of information already on woodcock, but is surely the equivalent of the French Woodcock Club, the CNB, it relation to its professionalism and national coverage. In the period 1991–92 to 2007–08, the NARGC examined 12,343 woodcock wings sent to them members from all parts of Ireland – see Table 2. This wing survey was used to age the woodcock shot by members and shows some interesting and unexpected results in relation to what some previous commentators on woodcock would have expected. From 1991 to 2004 the percentage of young woodcock in the gamebag returns from Irish shooters never exceeded 46.54%. However, since 2004 it has not dropped below 50.15% and, in the shooting season 2005–2006, the percentage of juveniles in the wing survey returns reached an all-time high of 56.00%. It can also be seen from Table 2 that the overall numberof birds shot has increased year on year since 1991–1992, with peaks of 1,406 in 1995–1996 and 1,025 in 1996–1997, 1,026 in 2005–2006 and a current all-time high of 1,570 in 2007–2008. This could, of course, simply be the result of greater shooting pressure or greater participation in the NARGC wing survey. Whichever is the case it remains, nevertheless, an important indication of what is happening in the world of woodcock hunting in the Irish Republic.

TABLE 2

Woodcock Wing Survey

SEASON	ADULT	YOUNG	TOTAL	% YOUNG
1991–1992	149	106	255	41.57
1992–1993	427	114	541	21.07
1993–1994	488	176	664	26.50
1994–1995	373	258	631	40.88
1995–1996	867	541	1,406	38.47
1996–1997	643	382	1,025	37.27
1997–1998	311	141	452	31.19
1998–1999	309	269	578	46.54
1999–2000	357	127	484	26.24
2000–2001	230	117	347	33.71
2001–2002	328	215	543	39.59
2002–2003	310	212	522	40.61
2003–2004	491	287	778	36.89
2004–2005	337	339	676	50.15
2005–2006	446	579	1,026	56.00
2006–2007	408	437	845	51.70
2007–2008	764	806	1,570	51.00

[National Association of Regional Game Councils Ireland 2008]

Two interesting facts arise here. For French scientists at the ONCFS these higher percentages above the 50% mark are indicative of increasing hunting pressure as more juveniles are seen to be 'fitting-in' to wintering sites vacated as a result of the adult occupants having been shot the previous season. I do, however, have my doubts in relation to how far we can accept this thesis as quite simply the young birds have to go somewhere and are not just filling empty locations. These high percentages of recorded juveniles fly in the face of accepted wisdom that far fewer juvenile birds migrate to our western extremities than adult woodcock do and that, therefore, the further west you shoot the lower the number of young birds you will encounter. The Irish survey casts serious doubts upon the validity of this premise. Colin McKelvie [1986: 134] suggested '...the further west we look in the woodcock's wintering range in the British Isles the lower the proportion of young birds'. This has seldom been my experience in a Welsh context and clearly the Irish figures show this to be fundamentally not the case. The wing analysis I carried out for the Welsh Woodcock Club in the period 2006–2009 shows the pattern indicated by Table 3.

TABLE 3

Welsh Woodcock Club Wing Analysis

SEASON	ADULT	JUVENILES
2006–2007	58%	42%
2007–2008	35%	65%
2008–2009	55%	45%

Moreover, my personal records from my game book over the ten years 1999–2009 show a predominant balance between adults and juveniles. In fact, in those instances where there is a drastic imbalance, it is towards juvenile woodcock by 70% and 80% respectively. In some bags I examined, the ratio was 9:1 in favour of juveniles.

Other than the 1992–1993, 1993–1994 and 1999–2000 seasons, where the percentage of juveniles was in the mid-20s, the Irish figures only fall below 32% in one year and for the rest of the period are in the high 30s to 40s. There appears to be a growing trend of juvenile woodcock migrating as far west as their adult counterparts, and in comparable numbers.

Across Europe, there is an utter lack of consistency in relation to protecting woodcock. In a joint paper with his colleague François Grossman ('A management plan for woodcock 2001'), Dr Yves Ferrand shows the haphazard situation that exists in the current 'unified' Europe. The hunting seasons vary from a start in August (Sweden and Finland) to a finish on 28th February in Greece and 30th April in Austria. It has been the case that, in Sweden, summer shooting can take place between the 25th June and 15th July: this arrangement was banned in 1995 and 1996 and reintroduced in 1997 and 1998. It is estimated that France, Greece and Italy between them account for 93% of the annual bag of woodcock. In these individual countries again the seasons vary. The French season runs from 1st September to 20th February, the Greek season from 15th September to 28th February and the Italian from 20th September to 31st January. In those countries of most interest to the British and French woodcock shooter, the hunting seasons clearly exploit the return of post-breeding woodcock. For example: Bellorussia 31st March to mid-April; Czech Republic 16th March to 15th April; Hungary 1st March to 10th April; Latvia 1st April to 10th May; Lithuania 1st April to 10th May; Poland 15th April to 15th May; Russia 1st April to 20th May.

Readers may take comfort from the fact that some of these countries are now members of the European Union and hopefully can be influenced not to 'shoot the seed corn'. However, what really drives the shooting on the breeding grounds during the initial phase of the breeding season is the affluence and unscrupulous nature of some European so-called sportsmen – a statement which reminds me of a most gruesome sight I was shown by French colleagues. A picture of 196 woodcock in neat rows! The result of one day's shooting, or slaughter, depending on how you view it. The original source of the photograph quite openly laid claim to other days like this on the Crimean Peninsula in May over the last four or five years. Excessively large bags are the norm. As far as I am aware, it is only FANBO and CNB that are kicking up a fuss here and applying political pressure via their governmental representatives. (I will be more than pleased to be shown to be absolutely wrong here, as UK-based shooting organisations rush to criticise me.)

Quite recently, the CNB successfully countered a move by the anti-blood sports fraternity to ban woodcock shooting in France – the antis claimed that numbers were extremely low – by producing its own data collected over the previous three decades. Can you imagine the amount of information we could amass in the UK? How much of it would be robust data? Very little, I would suggest. I have discussed this issue long and hard with colleagues, associates and friends in the woodcock shooting circles of the UK and Europe. I, like them, am surprised that the country which gave the world the cocker spaniel is bereft of its own Woodcock Shooters' Association or National Club. There is an obvious need for a UK/Republic of Ireland-wide association of woodcock shooters. This would be a threat to no one and would, I imagine, quite willingly work alongside other organisations. However, the particular focus of such a body is what would be significant, that being the shooting and conservation of woodcock.

Already, as stated, bag limits for woodcock have been introduced in some European countries. For example, across four 'regions' of Brittany (Morbihan, Finistere, Côtes d'Amor and Ille-et-Villane) there is now a weekly bag limit of three woodcock and a season's limit of thirty. Hunters there are issued with adhesive leg tags to be attached to each dead bird in their possession and, through a punch hole facility on their woodcock hunting licence, note the day, week and month of the season.

The question has to be whether there are any merits to imposing a bag limit on numbers of woodcock shot by individuals in the British Isles. The major problem would be one of enforcement. How would it be policed? In Brittany they have the advantage of game laws being enforced by rangers of the state-controlled Hunting and Wildlife Department, the ONCFS. Thus, the bag limit is enforced by state employees with the full might of the law behind them. However, I suspect that legal mechanisms relating to shooting seasons and broader field sports issues in the British Isles, as in France, work as the result of most hunters being honest and law-abiding citizens. Do we need such a mechanism in place, and what would its main benefit be?

My understanding is that, in Brittany, the main reason for introducing such a bag limit was primarily to severely restrict and, over time, dispense with, the activities of commercial woodcock shooting interests but, to a lesser extent, to curb the unacceptable over-exploitation by a minority of individuals. This initiative was, in fact, driven by the Club Nationale de Béccassiers, the French Woodcock Club. However, it is clearly the case that culture and tradition play an important part in ensuring that such a mechanism for controlling numbers shot is workable. For the French revere the woodcock, holding it in the highest esteem. So much so that the majority of French hunters only shoot woodcock over pointers or setters and, from January to the end of the season on the 20th February each dog, when hunting, is required by law to have a bell attached to its collar. From my experiences of engaging in this type of hunting in Brittany, many French hunters are more interested in the number of times their dogs go on point, so-called 'points achieved', in the one day than in bag numbers. In my experience, hunters of this calibre work easily within the bag limit restrictions. The majority of them only shoot at woodcock that have been 'pointed-up' by their dogs. They do not shoot at woodcock that are inadvertently flushed by dogs or Guns. During my visits to France these instructions were made abundantly clear on commencement of the day's shooting. Thus, many French sportsmen are loading the dice, as it were, firmly in the woodcock's favour. The bag limit is seen as a sensible conservationist's stance which adds to woodcock management techniques. However, we should be aware that hunting pressure on woodcock in France is far, far higher than it is in the British Isles.

From my perspective, the only possible reasons for introducing a bag limit on woodcock are the interlinked ones of over-exploitation and commercial exploitation of a truly wild resource. A bag limit would restrict the cull exercised by both the individual hunter and commercial set-ups. However, the main problem in the UK and Ireland is the absence of any validated bag numbers of woodcock, both for individual hunters and commercial operations. We have nothing to go on other than locally sourced rumours but, if they are anywhere near true, something needs to be done very soon. For, in comparison to the husbandry of the commercial pheasant or partridge shoot, commercial woodcock shooting is 'cost cheap' and 'profit large'! There are no feed costs, no medicated feed, no vermin control costs, no release pens to maintain and, for most commercial woodcock shoots (with some notable exceptions), very little in terms of habitat costs. However, close scrutiny of British and Irish game dealer's records would give a very good indication of how many woodcock are traded and where the big or excessive bags are coming from. In the winter of 2008–2009 woodcock were to be found on many game dealers' websites at the staggering price of £8.50 each. Couple this to a first-hand report I received from a game dealer, in early February 2008, of a shipment of 4,000 woodcock coming in from across the UK and Ireland and one can easily see this is a lucrative trade!

There is an apparently easy solution to this and that is to emulate the French by banning the sale of woodcock, introducing a bag limit which includes a set number of leg tags and also, to impose such restrictions as vigorously as we do in favour of sea trout and salmon. However, I cannot see that banning the sale of woodcock is the way forward. Nonetheless, given a mandatory bag limit of, say, three woodcock per week per Gun, the issue of over-exploitation by commercial operations is dealt a death blow. From experience, I am convinced this could work if it became law because I have every faith in the self-policing, law-abiding nature of the majority of British and Irish sporting individuals. In over forty years of formal participation in game angling associations, shooting clubs and shooting syndicates, examples of those who have broken the organisations' rules deliberately are in the overwhelming minority. I have little doubt that the shooting community would self-enforce, self-police such new laws – but are they really required? Consider this: in the 2007–2008 shooting season, six Guns shot a total of seven days driven woodcock between 27th December 2007 and 10th January 2008. Between them they shot 364 woodcock with a ratio of 80% juveniles in the bag. They averaged fifty-two per day or just fewer than eight per Gun. Is that acceptable to the shooting community? It certainly is not to me. The only reason I know this is because one of the Guns was stupid enough to phone me up to brag about it. As if this were not enough, he willingly offered up the fact that, on a separate day, he was one of a party of eight Guns who shot 126 woodcock that day.

The danger here is that we fall into the trap of not comparing like with like. Commercial shoots differ in terms of their approach and ethos to woodcock shooting. I have direct experience of only one such enterprise and that is the Eilean Iarmain shoot on Skye. Here, under the jurisdiction of Sir Iain Noble and controlled by Headkeeper Michael Mackenzie, the emphasis is on the quality of the sport and the testing nature of woodcock shooting in all its guises. Shooting days are organised to almost ensure that matters are heavily weighted in favour of the birds. Shooting woodcock at Eilean Iarmain is challenging, the sporting ethos is to the fore and one never feels that woodcock are being exploited as a cash crop. This, I suspect, is largely the result of my having only shot there as a walked-up Gun in a rough shooting sense where, at the end of a gruelling but ecstatic experience, one really felt that one had worked for one's sport. Woodcock shooting at Eilean Iarmain is not the mainstay of the estate's financial or business operations and is therefore run accordingly as a sporting experience, whereby woodcock are truly valued and not overly exploited.

My main problem with some commercial woodcock operations is that they do simply exploit the woodcock as a readily available cash crop. For, some of these operations start their day by dawn-flighting woodcock on their way back from nocturnal feeding forays on nearby pastureland, then follow this up with a day's shooting either driven or over pointers and then flight shoot woodcock in the evening on their way out to feed at dusk. There is little doubt that what attracts continental Guns from France, Italy, South Africa and even further afield is the fact that there

The author and Dr Jean Paul Boidot shooting woodcock in Brittany.

Woodcock heaven: The Eilean Iarmain Estate on the Isle of Skye.

is no bag limit and that large bags are frequently taken. One would have thought that by now, as exploitation of our sea fisheries, our salmon stocks and wildlife habitat are obvious and clearly understood, all participants would appreciate that we cannot simply take and take and take. I have little problem with the sensible and responsible harvesting of any resource. However, to shoot woodcock at dawn, during the day and again at dusk is literally a case of overkill.

Whilst flight shooting of woodcock at dusk is practised in England, Scotland and Wales it is illegal to do so in the Republic of Ireland. It is the case that, in England, Scotland and Wales, individual hunters and commercial set-ups engage in such activities. As such, whilst when doing so to the absolute letter of the law, nothing illegal is taking place, is it an acceptable practice? How sporting is it? Prior to my spat with the great Colin McKelvie I had never, in fact, participated in shooting woodcock flighting at dusk. Subsequent to that time I have only ever engaged in such practice on four occasions in two different venues. At Eilean Iarmain on the Isle of Skye I found it to be exceedingly difficult – it was, in fact, organised and arranged to present the most testing shots imaginable. All was stacked in the woodcock's favour! The Guns were positioned so that the woodcock came over them high and fast and presented only fleeting glimpses. It was very very difficult shooting indeed: I managed one woodcock for two evenings' flighting. Conversely, in lowland south-west Wales, standing in a clearing in a wooded valley, the birds could be seen coming a long way off and were relatively easy. I took two for two shots. On the basis of 'not knocking anything until you've tried it' I tried it and have not done so since. I can see the attraction of doing so, in the Scottish example of how it should be done, but really my heart is in the hunting of woodcock over good dogs and not in ambushing them at dusk. To each their own, but this practice is not for me. I derive enough pleasure and enough opportunities from hunting them in the day. Therefore, it would seem rather excessive to also target them at dawn and dusk.

Both my intellect and instinct tell me I am right to oppose such practice. Mike Swan of the Game and Wildlife Conservation Trust, who I know has a love and appreciation of woodcock equal to mine, summed up my feelings almost entirely when he suggested:

> In country where woodcock can be shot during the day by walking-up, shooting flight lines is probably greedy. You can hardly expect a wild resource like this to stand being worked twice [let alone three times – author's emphasis]. However, where there are large forestry blocks, or similar impossible cover, flight lines may be the only opportunity, and I see no harm in taking it. A word of warning should be sounded however. Woodcock flight lines are the most easily over-shot resource I know…Woodcock are wonderful birds and all the indications are that they are on the increase. Please do not abuse them.
>
> [Swan 1991: 86, 87]

I concur with my friend Mike Swan on all counts. I, too, am primarily interested in the holistic experience of hunting woodcock, not in exploiting them. Flight shooting of woodcock can be made to be extremely difficult and thus sporting, or ridiculously easy and thus bad practice. Mine is a personal choice, I have 'sucked it and seen it' but did not like the taste! Flight shooting of woodcock in comparison to days in the field holds no interest for me. I simply do not feel the need to shoot woodcock that badly!

As noted earlier, the French Woodcock Club is keen to limit the exploitation of woodcock by introducing bag limits. They have also set the banning of flight shooting of woodcock as one of their other main objectives and have fed these proposals into the EU Commission which drew up the 2006 and 2007 Draft Woodcock Management Plans. In fact they are diametrically opposed to the shooting of woodcock flighting at or just before dusk or dawn. This kind of shooting they term *'le tir à la passé'* [McKelvie 1987: 161]: derived from the Breton language it translates as 'pass-shooting'. It was made clear during my visit to Brittany that any flouting of this rule would result in me, the Gun, and my host being asked to leave the field. It was a hard time for a dyed-in-the-wool Welsh/Irish opportunist rough shooter like me as I inadvertently walked-up many woodcock on one visit to Brittany.

In fact, and quite surprisingly so, Colin McKelvie, whilst being a stout defender of shooting flighting woodcock, drew attention to the fact that in the UK, such practice is probably technically illegal:

> In the United Kingdom...woodcock flighting [the shooting of them – author's emphasis] at dusk has, strictly speaking, always been on the fringes of legality, since the law forbids the pursuit of game before one hour prior to sunrise and later [no later – author's correction] than one hour after sunset. Official sunset time comes long before the last of the light has gone, and when woodcock begin to flight out to feed on winter's evenings they may do so just as the clock should be telling the punctiliously law-abiding sportsman that they are no longer 'fair game'. Effective enforcement of this law is quite another matter...
>
> [McKelvie 1986: 162]

A very perceptive and knowledgeable Colin McKelvie is of course correct, as I have also indicated elsewhere in this book, that such laws need to be policed in order to be effective. However, from my point of view, whilst the legality of such practice is highly questionable and should be taken seriously, the easily overlooked yet resonant reference to 'Woodcock begin to flight out to feed on winter evenings...' does, in fact, deliver the moral death blow for such practice. I find it more and more abhorrent to accept that such a truly magnificent game bird, which offers such spectacular, exciting and rewarding sport in a walked-up hunting sense, should be shot in this manner having survived the day largely in those localities where the shooting of woodcock over dogs has already taken place.

While Colin McKelvie did not consider the shooting of flighting woodcock to be particularly damaging to overall woodcock numbers, he and I could never agree upon this. For, even when one is only standing under an evening flight path, to do so on a regular basis quickly results in fewer and fewer woodcock being counted at that location. In fact I often find it necessary to rest my counting places and shift operations elsewhere in the vicinity. Clearly, if Guns regularly occupy the same places from which to shoot woodcock they do not only kill some of them but also impact upon and alter the birds' preferred timetable and route to their feeding grounds. They shift their routes and come later. These birds are on their way to feed and should be left in peace to do so. To intercept and shoot them is unethical in my book, especially in those cases where money changes hands. When Guns are placed at such spots for the first time in a season, or after such spots have been well-rested, woodcock come confidently and relatively slowly, in an almost innocent manner. In such circumstances, shooting moths would be more sporting. Such practice is abhorrent to me. I have little doubt that, if allowed to continue, it will damage us all. What other game bird do we shoot flighting back to roost, or flighting out to feed?

I must admit that the only experience I have of driven woodcock shooting has been that of being put to 'stand' on a rough shooting day to intercept woodcock using the 'back door' as it were, or being put well forward of long and dense stretches of cover or strips of woodland. I infrequently accompany a group of three friends, one of whom is a lifelong friend of mine, who rough shoot together every Saturday as they have done for thirty years and more and who invariably organise their rough shooting for woodcock so that one or even two of them act as standing Guns around the back of the wood or at the far end of the long, big and thick hedges they love to work. All of this is done in a very informal manner and is good fun to boot. It is how rough shooters work for each other. It is the polar opposite of formal, commercial driven woodcock shooting, of which there are some vociferous critics:

> ...I strongly disapprove of large scale driving [of woodcock – author's emphasis] such as takes place on some of the commercial shoots. I see little sport in surrounding cover and then putting in...beaters and their dogs. Most of the time it is little more than a slaughter and unworthy of one of the most elusive and sporting of birds. The problem is that the clients of commercial shoots want big bags and have neither the inclination nor the stamina to shoot woodcock properly, by slogging the hard miles for a possible reward of no more than a couple of birds.
>
> [Butler 2006: 143]

Douglas Butler has the issue by the throat and is to be admired for his honest and frank stance. His condemnation of commercial woodcock shoots is based upon his experience of some such operations in the Republic of Ireland but could quite rightly be applied quite easily to commercial interests in the UK. Worryingly so, there is a growing trend of such commercial operations being set up in Wales, Scotland and England and of greater concern are the dark rumours of woodcock being persecuted. Douglas Butler echoes my sentiments entirely as I, too, strongly oppose such practices where woodcock are driven and driven and driven to produce high bag numbers and to appease guest Guns paying high fees. These practices are overwhelmingly profit driven and appear to show little care for the future of this great sporting bird. I am not aware of a single commercial woodcock shoot in the entire UK or Ireland that operates a mandatory bag limit. There should be – and we need it to happen sooner rather than later!

There are, nevertheless, responsible commercial woodcock shoots where the emphasis is upon what one might term a 'wild' day in the field and where not even an opportunity to shoot at a woodcock is guaranteed, let alone an estimated bag size to be anticipated. It is only fair that we acknowledge such practice.

Sadly, it is clearly the case that there are good commercial operations and bad commercial operations. As for the bad ones, they may just have enough time to clean-up their act and start to self-regulate before the EU decides for them and' effectively, puts them out of business. Commercial operations do, however, introduce new blood to the sport of woodcock shooting and could hopefully result in greater numbers of people having empathy with what is largely a minority pursuit. Those of us who have an abundance of woodcock shooting at our disposal really do need to recognise how fortunate we are and make an effort to introduce inexperienced Guns to our sport with woodcock and instil in them also an appreciation and love of woodcock.

Woodcock were made to be hunted but this should be done in a responsible manner. The long-term effects of high-pressure tactics can only be detrimental to woodcock numbers in a localised or regionalised sense. Again, the French method of estimating hunting pressure through ageing the woodcock shot may be useful here. Ideally, the ratio of young to adults should be as near to 50:50 as possible. The higher the ratio of juveniles in the bag, the greater the hunting pressure. It is suggested that higher numbers of juveniles shot is indicative of high numbers of adults shot the previous season, as the current season's young take over those places previously occupied by adult birds. In a localised sense one could measure this through well-documented records of particular shots, or areas even, where each bird shot was aged and then comparisons carried out in each subsequent season. However, I am not entirely convinced by this claim by the French. Young birds of the year have to go somewhere to roost and feed and thus they cannot all be occupying places vacated by adults that have been shot the previous season. Besides which, I frequently flush three, four and even six woodcock from patches of cover no more than 6 x 6 yards or so square. Ageing of woodcock is, nevertheless, important as it gives us an indication of how successful the previous breeding season was.

Having said that woodcock should be shot *responsibly*, I would like to comment upon a worrying trend on the British game shooting scene and that is the increasing fashion to ban the shooting of woodcock on organised shoots. The question is: why should anyone wish to ban woodcock shooting and, especially so, why is this drastic action being taken from within the game shooting fraternity itself? I do not hear fellow Guns calling for a halt to goose shooting or pigeon shooting or rabbit shooting or pheasant shooting – or any other quarry species for that matter. So why should we stop shooting woodcock and what are the reasons given? Those who cite conservation reasons in the context of wishing to increase local or pan-European numbers are simply deluding themselves. For, by the start of the main shooting season on an organised basis, mainly for pheasants, in late October and early November, any locally bred woodcock will have already shifted to new areas or regions of the British Isles as the genetic impulse for them to migrate, albeit internally to the UK and to and from Ireland, compels them to do so. Therefore, if woodcock were to be shot in late October or early November, they would be predominantly migrants from elsewhere in the British Isles – or Europe, even. In relation to these migrants from elsewhere in Europe a total ban on shooting them would have very little impact on overall numbers as there are so many other factors involved in their survival.

Those who would ban woodcock shooting on aesthetic grounds are beyond my help as the entire list of quarry species are equally attractive to me and, if this proposition is valid, logic dictates that for the same reason we should desist from shooting any species at all. A particularly annoying and stupid reason this – but one that people are free to exercise if they must. But are not all God's creatures wonderful in their own way, including the chickens, sheep and all the other animals and fowl that we harvest?

The proposition to ban woodcock shooting on conservation grounds is most dangerous to us as it implies that woodcock are in trouble in a sustainability sense. They are not! As I have painstakingly argued in this book, there is not a shred of scientific evidence to suggest that woodcock, as internal residents to the British Isles or across Europe, Scandinavia or north-west Russia, are in decline. In a letter to Jonathon Young, then editor of *The Field* magazine, which he shared with me, Colin McKelvie argued it was nonsense to stop shooting woodcock on conservation grounds:

> If woodcock are spared on sentimental grounds, because they're pretty birds, so be it. But if it's done on the assumption it is good conservation practice, bringing greater woodcock numbers in future seasons, it is simply fallacious and based on an ill-conceived grasp of woodcock ways. With shooting pressure having no proven effect on UK winter or spring numbers, it is frankly pointless.
>
> [McKelvie 2004]

Thus, the idea of stopping woodcock shooting on conservation grounds is based upon subjective criteria and not fact, and as such it is not only stupid but could adversely affect the rest of us.

Is there anything that flies better or tastes better than a woodcock? I have no qualms in reaping the bounty that is provided. I respect and love my woodcock. However, we all need to recognise how fragile a sporting gift woodcock are for us and not take them for granted. Since the start of the new millennium we have enjoyed some exceptional seasons. A trawl of reliable contacts across the UK, Ireland and north-west Europe shows that the majority of woodcock enthusiasts are convinced that numbers have increased or, at worst, are high. From countless discussions of the topic and from personal experience I have little doubt whatsoever that woodcock are on the increase. It has been notably the case that people of my generation, born in the 1940s and 1950s, have a tendency to describe many other present situations as worse than in their youth – whether that is salmon numbers, or the state of fish stocks at sea, or grouse populations – but the worst estimation for woodcock is that numbers are high and stable and the majority view of lifelong woodcock enthusiasts is that numbers have increased since their boyhood and young adulthood.

People say you never forget the first woodcock you shot. I am therefore an exception to this, as I have no real memory of when I shot my first, but I think it was when I was about fourteen. One of my uncles had all the rough shooting gear you could imagine, including a very nice English side-by-side by, I seem to recall, Harrison and Hussey. However, he preferred to work his ferrets and as I became a 'trusted' and safe member of the team he would hand over his gun to me. My father bought me my first shotgun at sixteen and I do know that, by that time, I had shot several woodcock, so my first must have been taken between the ages of fourteen and sixteen. That was many years ago and whilst I do not exactly recall the demise of my first woodcock – which, in a family of four ardent woodcock hunting adults, was applauded but did not go down in the family's history of the family – I clearly remember those days and seasons of woodcock hunting. It is no flight of sentimentality or nostalgia, because I know we encountered fewer woodcock then than now! Those were days of jubilation when perhaps six or eight were flushed as a part of a rough shooting day and two or three ended up in the bag. We were mad keen on our woodcock shooting and took every opportunity to enjoy our sport with them but numbers-wise, there were simply nowhere near as many as I encounter today. I have several friends who are also third generation woodcock hunters from similarly sized families of dedicated hunters and they, too, see the woodcock as having significantly increased in numbers.

Conclusion

I do see the future for woodcock as comparatively positive but, as mentioned previously, there are a number of caveats. Despite the fact that they are plentiful, they remain a fragile hunting resource.

One reason for their fragility is that they are comparatively easily affected by adverse weather conditions. At one end of the weather extremes, that of extreme cold weather, we can – and have in fact – put measures in place to protect them from exploitation when at their most vulnerable, that being the mandatory protracted cold-weather ban as practised in the UK and emulated now in France. However, at the other end of the weather extreme – that of drought – there is little that we mere mortals can do in the short term. The main threat here lies in the increasing incidence of drought conditions in the general region of the breeding grounds, which greatly increases mortality rates amongst woodcock broods. I have in this book presented some of the facts that hint at global warming and climatic change already affecting woodcock behaviour; for example, recent years when significant numbers of Russian-bred woodcock simply stayed put in the forests there until late November and December, also, of the woodcock's breeding range expanding northwards over the last two to three decades. This warming-up effect is a very real threat to woodcock and also to those of us in north-west Europe who depend so heavily for our sport on migratory woodcock.

The other major concern I harbour is the potentially disastrous impact that the worst side of the growing commercial woodcock shooting industry may have on our woodcock stocks if left to exploit them at current rates. A wild species such as woodcock, which ultimately depends upon itself and the vagaries of nature for its survival, cannot be expected to withstand such pressure and will undoubtedly go into decline. Those areas currently over-exploited for woodcock will, over time, become devoid of acceptable numbers of migratory woodcock. The analogy is that of eating the seed corn!

My conviction is that it is a privilege to hunt and shoot woodcock and that we must protect this as a part of our sporting heritage. Such an ethos is well understood in the Celtic fringes of Brittany, Wales and Ireland. Such woodcock hunting in wild, barren and hard places, which requires only that one has enough enthusiasm, stamina and good dogs, has been that of the common man for a very long time and has not depended upon status or wealth. This is to be seen clearly in Ireland, with its prolific numbers of local Game Clubs and Regional Game Councils, but more starkly through their response to and estimation of commercial woodcock operators. Such unease and opposition finds resonance in Wales and Scotland also. There is no room in this ethos for those who would make a quick profit out of a truly magnificent but vulnerable

The next generation: Jacob Trotman and Molly. The gun is, of course, empty!

migratory sporting bird and endanger its very survival. Such practices must not be tolerated and it falls upon those of us who care enough to persuade others who care little to join us in protecting the woodcock for future generations to appreciate. Sensible and respectful harvesting of woodcock is to be encouraged and enjoyed, as it is one of our birthrights. Commercial destruction of fragile wild species must be resisted at all costs. Woodcock shooting is not and cannot be allowed to become a numbers game, whether that implies bag sizes or pounds sterling or dollars. For some commercial woodcock shoots, bag sizes – the bigger the better and cash in the bank – represent 'joined-up thinking'. There is, of course, much work to do here in relation to re-educating those guilty of such practice.

Fortunately, there are sufficient numbers of individual Guns, groups of Guns, club shoots and even some commercial operators from whom they can learn. I have come across numerous examples of individuals and club members who impose restrictions on numbers shot and even introduce their own hard-weather bans, outside of the officially imposed ones, if they think weather conditions are having an effect on woodcock in the locality. These people are, of course, true sportsmen in the purest definition of the phrase. They are the polar opposites of the unethical 'get rich quick' wide boys. The so-called sportsmen, those visitors who pay high fees to indulge their greed and get their fix through shooting excessive numbers of woodcock, are also in dire need of some frank, adult education. Without their money, the game would be up!

However, it is, I am convinced, possible to persuade these people to adopt sensible and conservation-focused practices. Consider the growth in 'catch and release' of wild salmon and other migratory and resident game fish the world over. In a shooting context, there are voluntary codes of practice in relation to wild geese in Scotland which are applied by the guides themselves. Visiting Guns know what to expect, in that their bags will be limited, but still turn up in significant numbers. Those who can, travel the globe to catch and release all manner of sporting quarry, or to hunt under strict licences which control numbers of particular species shot.

It is of course possible to apply such restrictions to woodcock. Visiting Guns must learn and accept that the opportunity to shoot a woodcock is a very special event and not one based on how many you shoot. We must not continue to treat them as we would vermin. Imagine a winter landscape devoid of woodcock or containing so few it was hardly worth the bother. Imagine some of the truly inspiring or well-loved places you currently hunt, empty of woodcock. Imagine setting forth for a rough shooting day on a cold winter's morning after several days of frost with no expectation of woodcock in the bag whatsoever – or being restricted from shooting any because numbers were so low. Imagine a countryside which has lost that heart-stopping whirr of wings as a woodcock, a beautiful woodcock, erupts from the cover. Over to you!

Bibliography

Alexander, W. B. [1939], *The Woodcock in the British Isles*, British Trust for Ornithology, Oxford.
Ammann, G. A. [1977], 'Banding woodcock broods', Michigan Department of Natural Resources, Wildlife Division, USA.

Barrington, R. M. [1900], *Migration of Birds at Irish Light Stations*, Porter, London.
Berlich, H. D. [1989], 'Bone injuries and skeletal abnormalities in woodcock', Tierarzti Prax, Vol. 17, Issue 3, pp. 285–92, Giessen University, Germany.
Boidot, J. P. and Cau, J. F. [2006], 'Assessment of the abundance of woodcock over the last ten hunting seasons in France', in Yves Ferrand [ed], Sixth European Woodcock and Snipe Workshop – Proceedings of an International Symposium of the Wetlands International Woodcock and Snipe Specialist Group, Nantes, France 2003.
Butler, D. [2006], *Rough Shooting in Ireland*, Merlin Unwin Books, Shropshire, England.

Catlin, C. [2007], *The Game Book*, Swan Hill Press, Shrewsbury, England.
Churchill, R. [1925], *How to Shoot – Some Lessons in the Science of Shot Gun Shooting*, Geoffrey Bles, London.
Cooper, R. T., et al. [2008], 'American woodcock population status 2008', US Fish and Wildlife Department, Fort Snelling, USA.

Dennis, R. [2009], Highland Foundation for Wildlife website.
De Visme Shaw, L. H., et al. [1903], *Snipe and Woodcock*, Longmans, Green and Co., London.
Dobrynia, I. N. and Kharitonov, S. P. [2006], *The Russian Waterbird Migration Atlas: Temporal variation in migration routes in waterbirds around the world*, eds G.C. Boere et al., Edinburgh.

Duriez, O., et al. [2005], 'Wintering behaviour and spatial ecology of Eurasian woodcock *Scolopax rusticola* in western France', Ibis 147, France.
—— 'Habitat selection of the Eurasian woodcock in winter in relation to earthworm availability', Biological Conservation, France.

Felix, J. [2009], '*Scolopax rusticola* without frontiers', (self-published report), Spain.

Ferrand, Y. [1993], 'A census method for roding Eurasian woodcock in France', in J.R. Longcore and G.F. Sepik [eds], 'Proceedings of the 8th American Woodcock Symposium pp. 19–25, USFWS Report 16, Washington.

Ferrand, Y. and Gossman, F. [2001], 'Elements for a woodcock (*Scolopax rusticola*) management plan', Game and Wildlife Scientific Publications, ONCFS, France.

Ferrand, Y., et al. [2008], 'Monitoring of the wintering and breeding woodcock populations in France', Ornithos, France.
—— 'Monitoring of wintering and breeding woodcock populations in France', Revista Catalana d'Ornitologia 24:44—52, Spain.

Fragugoline, D. [1979], *La Bécasse des Bois*, Bordeaux.

Gossman, F., Ferrand, Y., et al. [2000], 'Ringing of woodcock in Russia from 1991 to 1997', in H. Kalchreuter [ed], Fifth European woodcock and snipe workshop, proceedings of an international symposium of the Wetlands International Woodcock and Snipe Specialist Group, Poland 1998.

Hirons, G. J. M. and Bickford-Smith, P. [1983], 'The diet and behaviour of Eurasian woodcock wintering in Cornwall', in proceedings of the Second European Snipe and Woodcock Workshop, IWRB.

Hoodless, A. [2002], *Migration Atlas*, Helm Publishers, London.
—— [2003], *Breeding Woodcock Survey 2003*, Game Conservancy Trust, Fordingbridge, Hampshire.
—— [2007], 'Habitat selection and foraging behaviour of breeding Eurasian woodcock *Scolopax rusticola*: a comparison between contrasting landscapes', British Ornithologists Union, United Kingdom.
—— 'The woodcock migration appeal', Game and Wildlife Conservation Trust, Hampshire, England.

Iljinsky, I. [2007], 'Woodcock recoveries in north-west Russia', Russian Ringing Federation, Russia.

Landsborough, Thompson A. [1929], 'The migration of British and Irish woodcock', *British Birds*, Vol. 23, London.

McKelvie, C. L. [1990], *The Book of the Woodcock*, (revised ed), Swan Hill Press, Shrewsbury, England. (First edition published by Debretts 1986.)
—— [2004] Article in *The Field* magazine, London.

National Association of Regional Game Councils Ireland [2008], *Woodcock Wing Survey* 1991–2008, Dublin, Ireland.

Saari, L. [2006], 'Spread of the woodcock *Scolopax rusticola* to Finnish Lapland', Wetlands International Woodcock and Snipe Study Group Newsletter, No. 32.
Schenk, J. [1927], 'The migration of woodcock in Europe', *British Birds*, Vol 19, London.
Seigne, J. W. [1936], *Woodcock*, Sportsman's Library, England.
Shorten, M. [1974], 'The European woodcock (*Scolopax rusticola*) a search of the literature since 1940', Game Conservancy Trust, Hampshire, England.
Smith, M. [1998], *Working Springers and Cockers*, self-published, England.
Snow, D. W. and Perrins, C. M. [1998], *The Birds of the Western Paleartic (concise edition)*, Oxford.
Swan, M. [1991], *Rough Shooting*, Swan Hill Press, Shrewsbury, England.

Thompson, W. [1849–1851], *The Natural History of Ireland Volumes 1–3*, Boehn, London.

Ussher, R. J. [1903], 'Snipe and woodcock in Ireland', in L. H. de Visme Shaw [1903] *Snipe and Woodcock*, Longmans, Green and Co., London.

Yarrel, W. [1843], *The History of British Birds, Volume 2*, London.

Index

Page numbers in *italic* refer to captions.

ageing woodcock 41–5, 164
American woodcock 21, 22, 49
anti-blood sports movement 154
associations and clubs 13, 18, 143–4, 155
Austria 154
Azores 48

bag limits 90, 104, 148, 155, 156, 161, 163
bag numbers 146, 148, 151, 152, 156, 157
ban on sale of woodcock 156
ban on shooting woodcock 164–5
  hard-weather bans 167, 169
Belgium 62
Bellorussia 154
Boidot, Dr Jean Paul 13, 38, 75, 112–13, 122, 141, 144, 149, *158*
boots and wellingtons 123

calls 32–3
camouflage 28, 93
Canary Islands 49
cartridges 111–12
Celtic names for woodcock 9
chicks 33–4
  carrying 33–4
  ringing 24
climate change 28, 49–50, 70, 139, 140–1, 142, 143, 149, 167
clothing 122–4
Club Nationale de Bécassiers (CNB) 17–18, 57, 143–4, 154, 155, 161
cocker spaniels 97, 99, 102, 146
colouration 35–7, *35*, *36–7*

commercial shoots 143, 149, 155, 156, 157, 159, 163–4, 167, 168–9
conservation issues 13, 17, 18, 143, 150, 165
  see also climate change; habitat loss/degradation; over-exploitation; population numbers
courtship 32–3
Czech Republic 154

Denmark 61, 68
ditches 90–1
dogs 94–110
  aggression 101
  bedding 106
  belling 103, 104, 155
  buying 99, 101
  choice of breed 97, 99, 101–3
  desired characteristics 99, 100, 101, 110
  field trials 99, 100
  GPS collars 103
  kennelling 106
  training 94–5, 96, 100–1
  transporting 106
  undisciplined 94, 101
  water work 95–6
driven woodcock shooting 121, 122, 162–3
dusky/rufous woodcock 21

earthworms 29, 89, 142, 149
eggs 33
European Federation of National Woodcock Shooting Clubs (FANBO) 13, 18, 144, 154

European Union Draft Management Plan for Woodcock 17, 18
European/Eurasian woodcock 11–12, 21, 22–3, 28–9, 49

fall of woodcock 121
feeding habits 20, 28–9, 89
Fennoscandia 61, 62, 70
Ferrand, Dr Yves 17, 26, *61*, 75, 141, 154
Finland 31, 46, 63, 70, 154
flight lines 27, 92, 160
flight shooting 121, 157, 159–62
forestation initiatives and projects 144–5, 146–7
France 62, 69, 72, 139, 141, 154
   hunting practices 103–5, 155–6
   research and monitoring programmes 17–18, 26–7, 69, 139, 140–1, 143–4, 148–9
French Woodcock Club see Club Nationale de Bécassiers (CNB)
French–Russian Woodcock Research Project 139, 140–1, 149

Game and Wildlife Conservation Trust (GWCT) 46, 150
game law enforcement 155, 157, 162
gamekeeper's waistcoat 123–4
geographical range 27–8
Gerald Cambrensis 9
Germany 61
gloves 124
gorse 91–3, 92
Gray, Robert 14, 80–1, 82, 83–8
Greece 154
guns 110–13
   Beretta Ultralight Deluxe 110, 113
   cartridges 111–12
   chokes 110, 112
   over and unders 110, 115
   side-by-sides 110, 115
   weight 110, 115

habitat loss/degradation 28, 143, 144, 149
hedges 90
Hinge, Mark 117, 125
Hoodless, Dr Andrew 23, 46, 52, 68
Hungary 154
hunting pressure 147–8, 149, 153, 154, 156, 164
hunting seasons 154, 155

Ireland 7, 46–8, 55, 56, 63, 64–5, 69, 70, 71, 145, 147, 151–2, 168
Irish setters 101–3
isotope analysis 46, 68
Italy 154

juvenile woodcock 41–2, 43, 44, 45, 50, 141, 152, 153, 164

Lapland 27–8
Latvia 154
leg injuries 38–41, *38–40*
Lithuania 154
longevity 55, 60

McKelvie, Colin 14, 30, 31, 41, 61, 63, 101, 113, 147, 153, 161–2, 165
Madeira 49
migrant woodcock 46–73
   arrival of 10–11, 14, 17, 49, 69–70, 72
   destination choice 50
   local and regional shifts 10, 24, 54, 55, 71, 74–5
   migration distances 51–3, 56–7, 58, 59, 63
   migration routes 46–9, 58–9, 65–6, 68–9, *71*
   migration triggers 61
   navigation 50
   numbers of see population numbers
   regions of origin 27, 46, 49, 61, 62–3
   resting places 63, 64, 65, 69
   small group migration 50, 51
   timing of migration 49–50
   transatlantic 49
   wintering grounds 10, 50, 62, 70, 144–5
moluccan woodcock 21
mud plaster casts 38–41, *38–40*

nest sites 24–5, 33
Netherlands 62
netting woodcock 20
North Sea Bird Club 63–4
Norway 62, 70, 139

over-exploitation 143, 149, 156–7, 159, 167

photoperiod 61
plumage 28
   feathers, uses for 138

see also colouration; wing analysis
Poland 154
population numbers 25–8, 139–40, 143
　American woodcock 22
　assessment methods 10, 12, 19, 23, 24–5, 26–7
　French monitoring 17–18, 26–7, 69, 143–4, 148–9
　UK monitoring 23–4, 25–6
　upward trend 12, 13, 17, 19, 22–3, 26, 27–8, 88, 150, 151, 166
　Woodcock Inquiry (1934–35) 25
predators 35

recipes 125–38
　Centenary Woodcock 134–5
　Cockbean Smoking 128–9
　CT's Easy Cook Woodcock 137
　Peacock Soup 136
　Smokecock 130–1
　Woodpecker Woodcock 126–7
　W.W.W. Game 132–3
reproduction 32–4
ringing woodcock 20–1, 60–1, *61, 62*, 148
　chicks 24
　private ringing schemes 54, 55–6, 61
　Russian programme 67
roding 17, 32
roosting places 89, 90, 145
Russia 31, 46, 48, 49, *61, 62*, 63, 65, 66–7, 70, 139, 140, 144, 149, 154

satellite tracking 53, 56–7, 58, 60, 67, 68
Scolopax minor see American woodcock
Scolopax rochussenii see moluccan woodcock
Scolopax rusticola see European/Eurasian woodcock
Scolopax saturata see dusky/rufous woodcock
Scotland 30, 47, 57–8, 62, 145, 146, 147
Scottish Woodcock Club 13, 18
sexing woodcock 34–5
shooting woodcock 74–88
　companions 93–4
　driven shoots 121, 122, 162–3
　exclusive woodcock shooting 75–6

　hunting grounds 77–9, 82–3, 89–93, 145–6
　philosophy of 14–16, 21, 75–6, 77–80
　'right and left' 117–22
　techniques 115–17
　the shooting experience 80–8
　weather patterns and 74
　wounded birds 113–14
short-billed woodcock 29–32, *30, 31*
softwood plantations 144–6
Spanish Woodcock Club 57
species of woodcock 21, 22
springer spaniels 97, 99, 100, 102, 146
sprockers 97, 99
Swan, Mike 160
Sweden 62, 70, 154

upland areas 93, 142
Ural Mountains 49, 62, 63, 70
urban woodcock 72–3
Ussher, Richard J. 9, 47, 48, 69

Wales 56, 69, 70, 141–2, 146–7
weight 21, 22, 28
Welsh Woodcock Club 13, 18, 19, 50
white woodcock 35, *36*, 56
wing analysis 26, 42–5, *42–4*, 152, 153
wintering grounds 10, 50, 62, 70, 144–5
woodcock
　attributes 28–9, 35–7, *35, 36–7*
　diet and feeding habits 20, 28–9, 89
　distribution (UK) 23
　in early history 9
　geographical range 27–8
　habitat 20, 89, 147
　habits 20, 29, 32–4, 88, 89
　longevity 55, 60
　reproduction 32–4
　resident populations 27, 55
　size and weight 21, 22, 28
　species of woodcock 21, 22
　see also migrant woodcock; population numbers
Woodcock Association of Ireland 13, 18
woodcock shooting estates 25–6, 56
woodcock-holding areas 77–9, 82–3, 89–93, 145–6
wounded birds 38–41, *38–40*, 113–14